CHART

IMITATES LIFE

BY
BRENDAN LEONARD

DO YOU EVER THINK ABOUT HOW
FUNNY AND STRANGE OUR LIVES ARE AS
HUMAN BEINGS IN THE 21ST CENTURY?

I DO. A LOT. SOMETIMES, I TRY TO MAKE
SENSE OF IT BY MAKING A GRAPH, DOODLE,
OR CHART ABOUT THE THINGS WE DO.

THIS BOOK IS A COLLECTION OF THOSE
DRAWINGS. I HOPE IT MAKES YOUR LIFE
A LITTLE MORE FUN. OR AT LEAST HELPS
YOU LAUGH AT THE ABSURDITY OF IT
A LITTLE BIT.

BRENDAN LEONARD
@SEMI_RAD

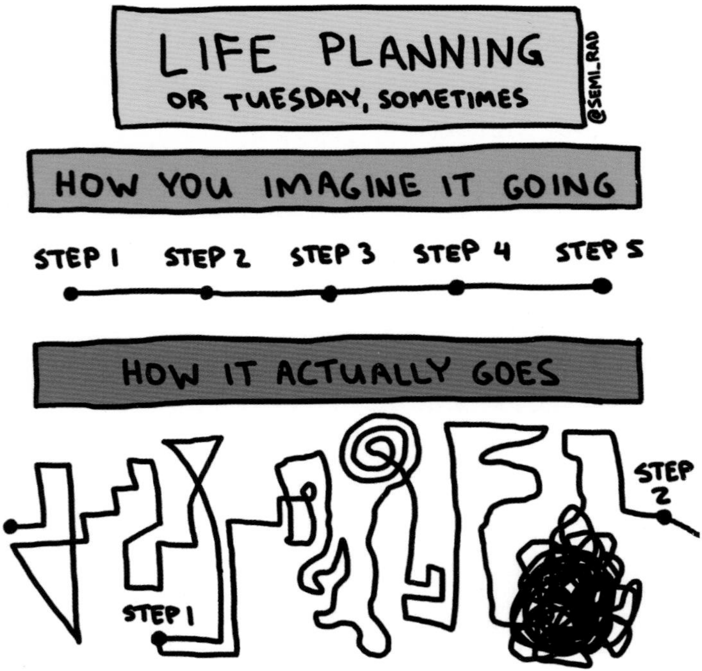
LIFE PLANNING
OR TUESDAY, SOMETIMES
@SEMI_RAD
HOW YOU IMAGINE IT GOING
STEP 1
STEP 2
STEP 3
STEP 4
STEP 5
HOW IT ACTUALLY GOES
STEP 1
STEP 2

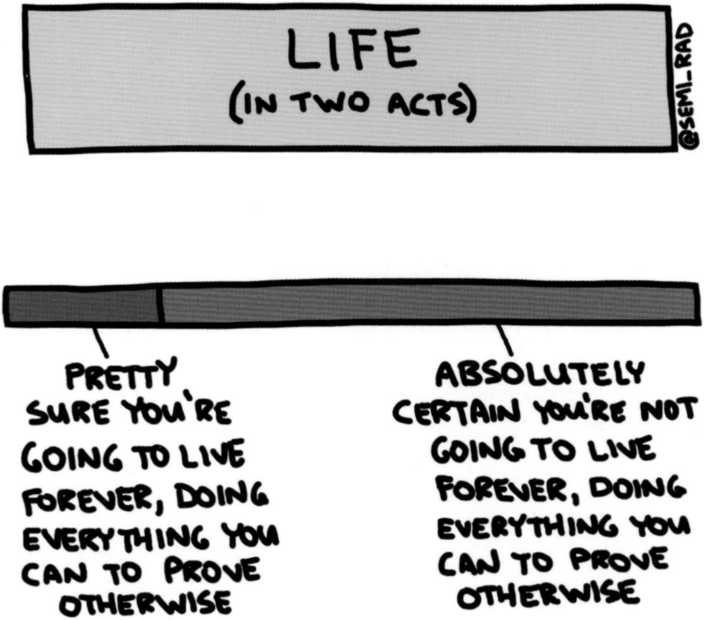
LIFE
(IN TWO ACTS)
@SEMI_RAD
PRETTY SURE YOU'RE GOING TO LIVE FOREVER, DOING EVERYTHING YOU CAN TO PROVE OTHERWISE
ABSOLUTELY CERTAIN YOU'RE NOT GOING TO LIVE FOREVER, DOING EVERYTHING YOU CAN TO PROVE OTHERWISE

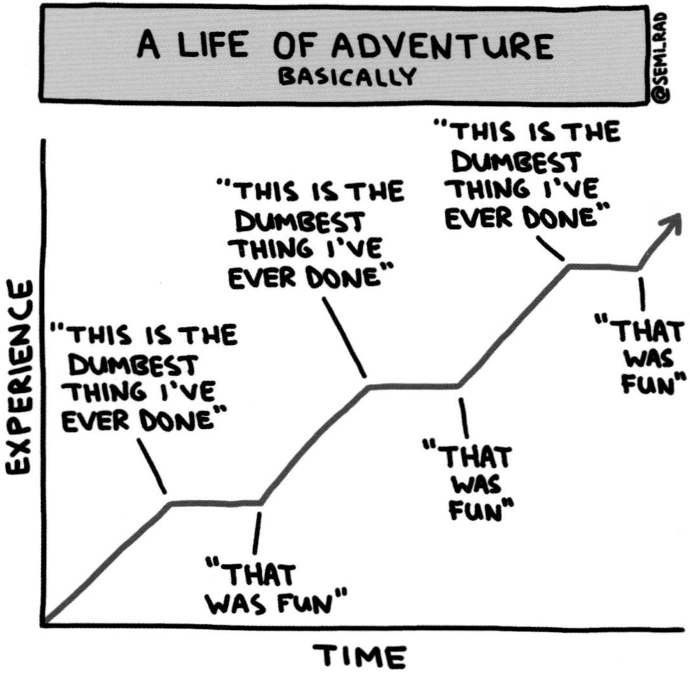
A LIFE OF ADVENTURE
BASICALLY
@SEMI.RAD
EXPERIENCE
TIME
"THIS IS THE DUMBEST THING I'VE EVER DONE"
"THAT WAS FUN"
"THIS IS THE DUMBEST THING I'VE EVER DONE"
"THAT WAS FUN"
"THIS IS THE DUMBEST THING I'VE EVER DONE"
"THAT WAS FUN"

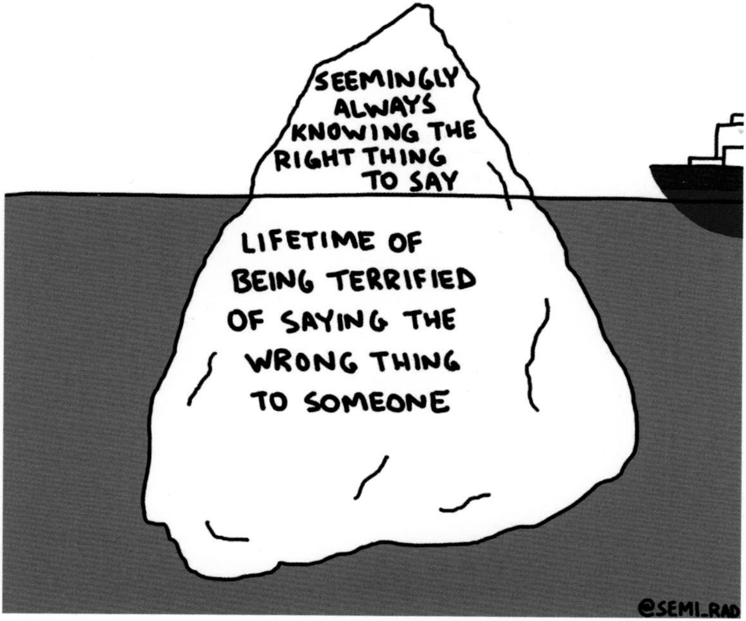
SEEMINGLY ALWAYS KNOWING THE RIGHT THING TO SAY
LIFETIME OF BEING TERRIFIED OF SAYING THE WRONG THING TO SOMEONE
@SEMI_RAD

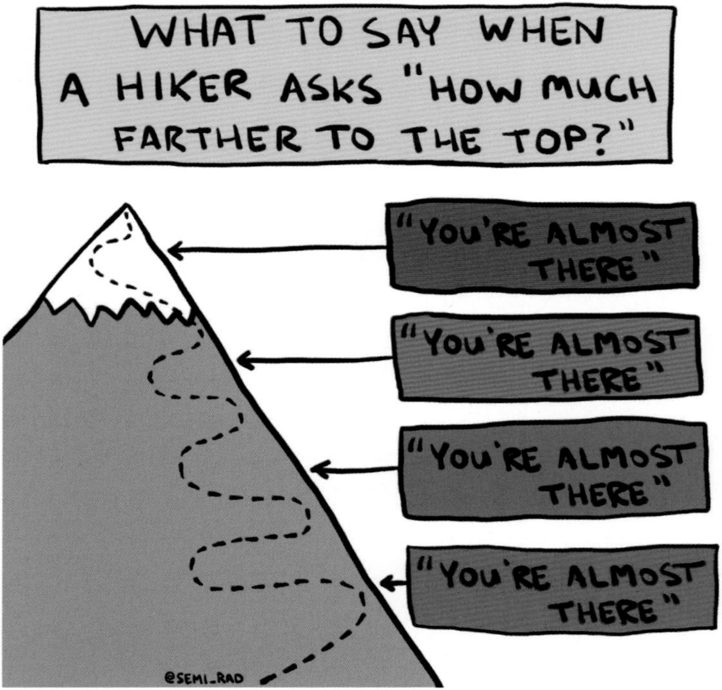
WHAT TO SAY WHEN A HIKER ASKS "HOW MUCH FARTHER TO THE TOP?"
"YOU'RE ALMOST THERE"
"YOU'RE ALMOST THERE"
"YOU'RE ALMOST THERE"
"YOU'RE ALMOST THERE"
@SEMI_RAD

HOW TO SAY GOODBYE TO FRIENDS AND FAMILY
(ACCORDING TO MY LIFE)

@SEMI_RAD

1. SAY THANKS, ACKNOWLEDGE THAT THIS WAS FUN
2. HUG
3. TALK ABOUT THE NEXT TIME YOU MIGHT SEE EACH OTHER
4. CRACK A JOKE AND/OR START YET ANOTHER CONVERSATION
5. AFTER FIVE MINUTES OF TALKING, REPEAT STEPS 1-5

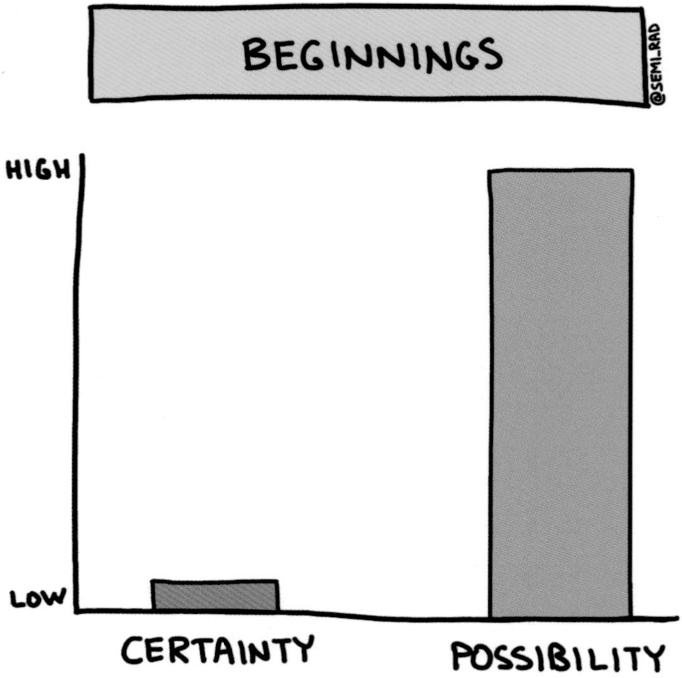
BEGINNINGS
@SEMI_RAD
HIGH
LOW
CERTAINTY
POSSIBILITY

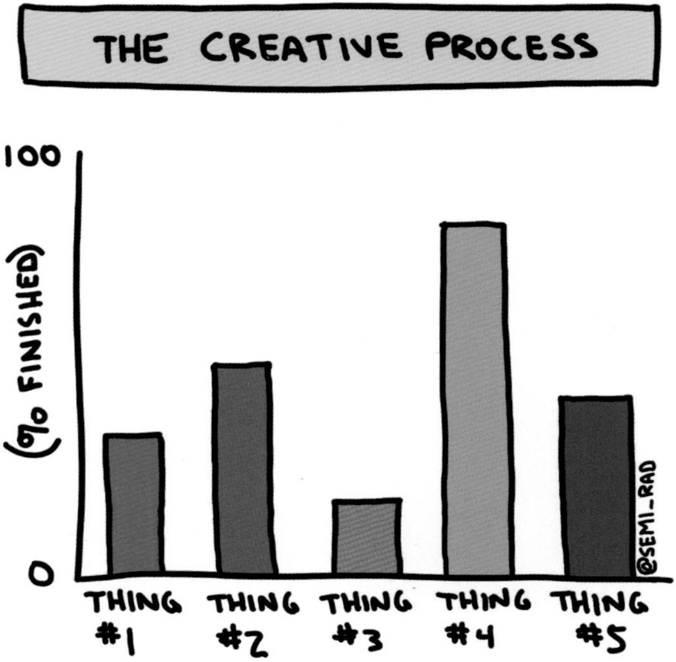
THE CREATIVE PROCESS
100
(% FINISHED)
0
THING #1
THING #2
THING #3
THING #4
THING #5
@SEMI_RAD

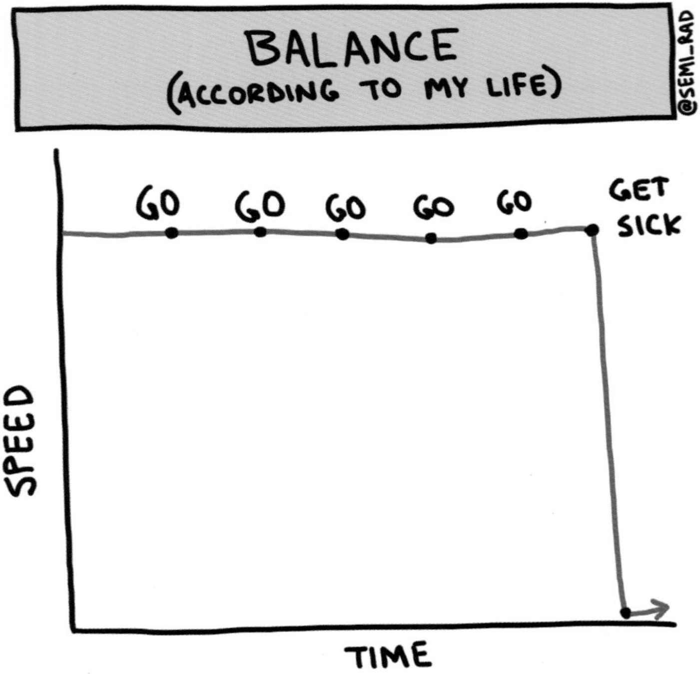
BALANCE
(ACCORDING TO MY LIFE)
@SEMI_RAD
GO
GO
GO
GO
GO
GET SICK
SPEED
TIME

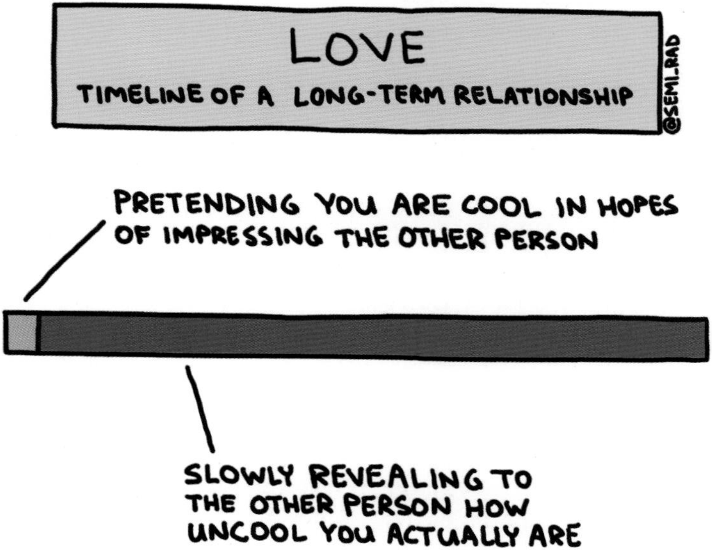
LOVE
TIMELINE OF A LONG-TERM RELATIONSHIP
@SEMI_RAD
PRETENDING YOU ARE COOL IN HOPES OF IMPRESSING THE OTHER PERSON
SLOWLY REVEALING TO THE OTHER PERSON HOW UNCOOL YOU ACTUALLY ARE

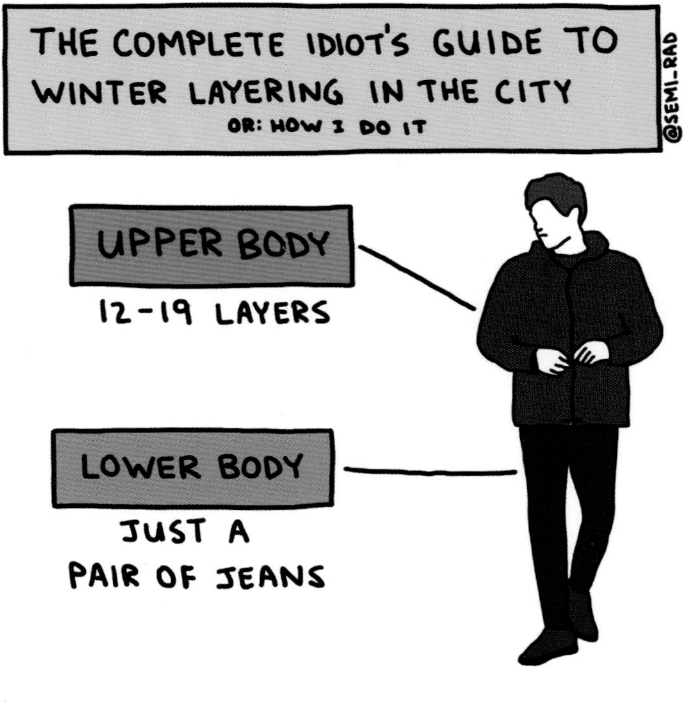

THE COMPLETE IDIOT'S GUIDE TO WINTER LAYERING IN THE CITY

OR: HOW I DO IT

@SEMI_RAD

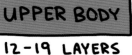

UPPER BODY

12-19 LAYERS

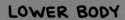

LOWER BODY

JUST A
PAIR OF JEANS

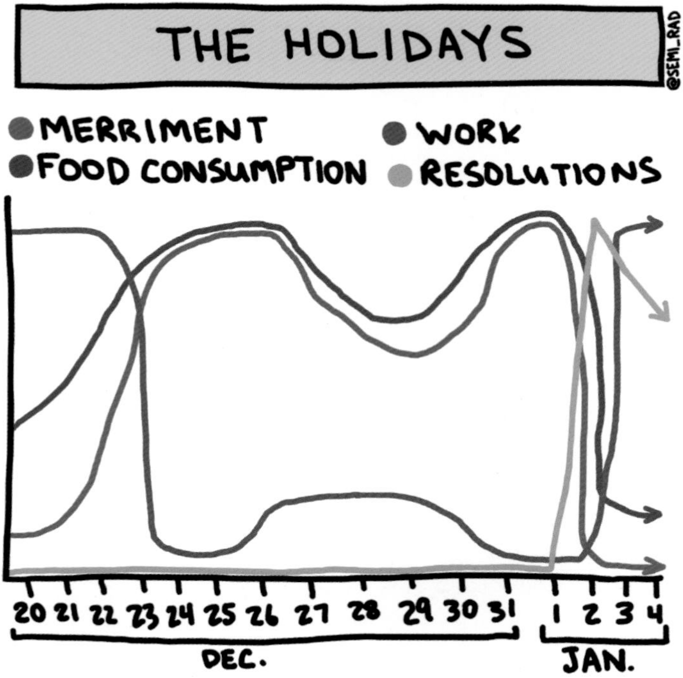
THE HOLIDAYS
@SEMI_RAD
MERRIMENT
WORK
FOOD CONSUMPTION
RESOLUTIONS
20 21 22 23 24 25 26 27 28 29 30 31
1 2 3 4
DEC.
JAN.

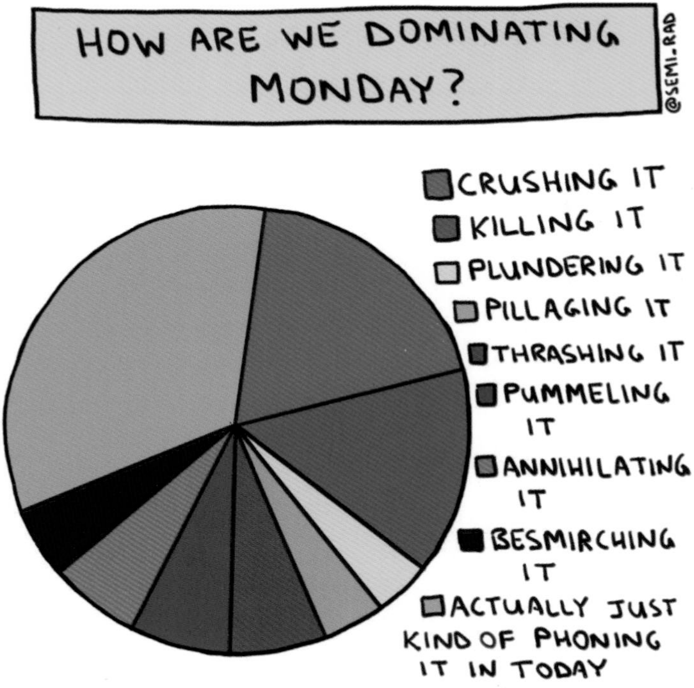
HOW ARE WE DOMINATING MONDAY?
@SEMI_RAD
CRUSHING IT
KILLING IT
PLUNDERING IT
PILLAGING IT
THRASHING IT
PUMMELING IT
ANNIHILATING IT
BESMIRCHING IT
ACTUALLY JUST KIND OF PHONING IT IN TODAY

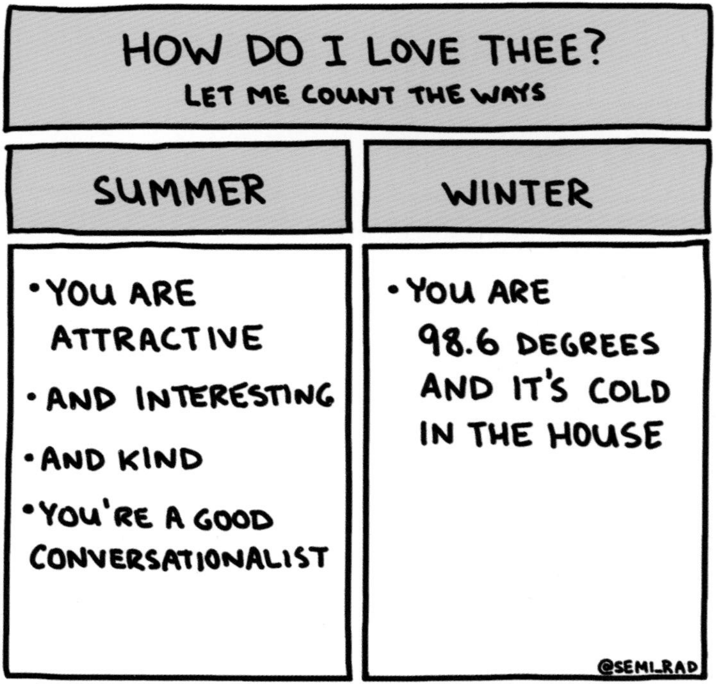
HOW DO I LOVE THEE?
LET ME COUNT THE WAYS
SUMMER
WINTER
• YOU ARE ATTRACTIVE
• AND INTERESTING
• AND KIND
• YOU'RE A GOOD CONVERSATIONALIST
• YOU ARE 98.6 DEGREES AND IT'S COLD IN THE HOUSE
@SEMI.RAD

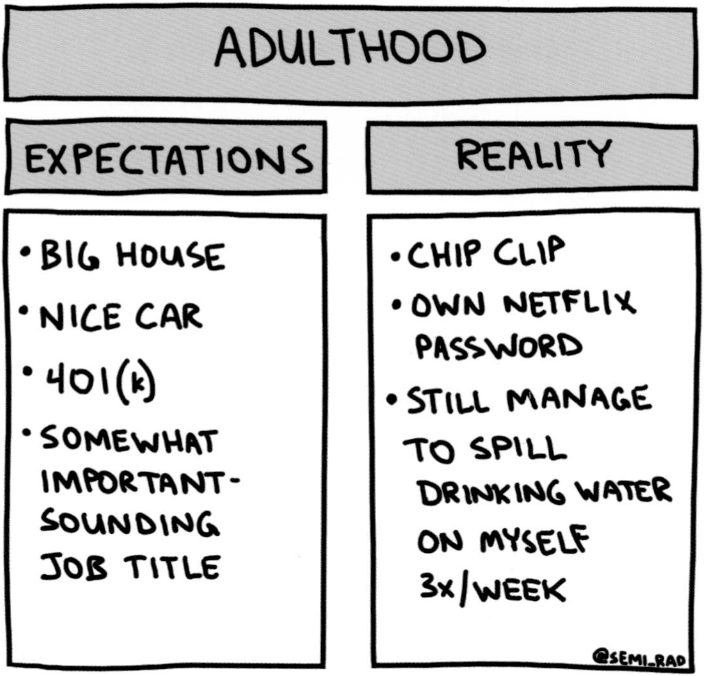
ADULTHOOD
EXPECTATIONS
REALITY
• BIG HOUSE
• NICE CAR
• 401(k)
• SOMEWHAT IMPORTANT-SOUNDING JOB TITLE
• CHIP CLIP
• OWN NETFLIX PASSWORD
• STILL MANAGE TO SPILL DRINKING WATER ON MYSELF 3x/WEEK
@SEMI_RAD

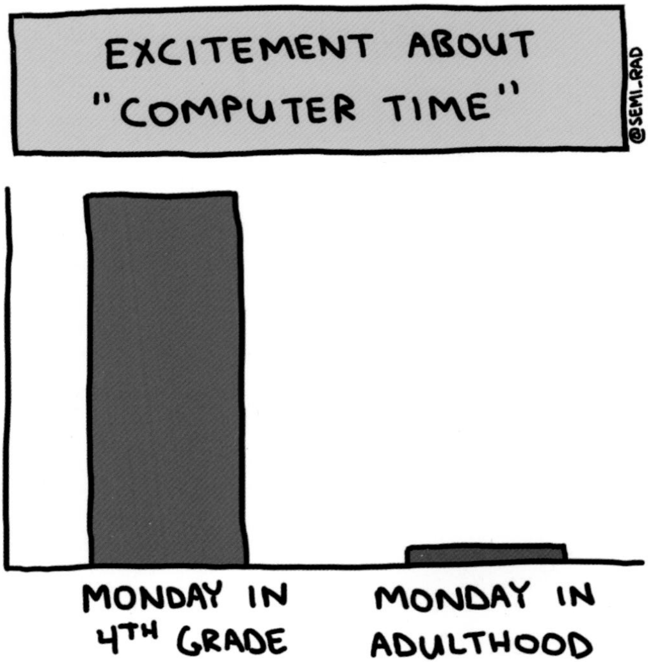
EXCITEMENT ABOUT "COMPUTER TIME"
@SEMI_RAD
MONDAY IN 4TH GRADE
MONDAY IN ADULTHOOD

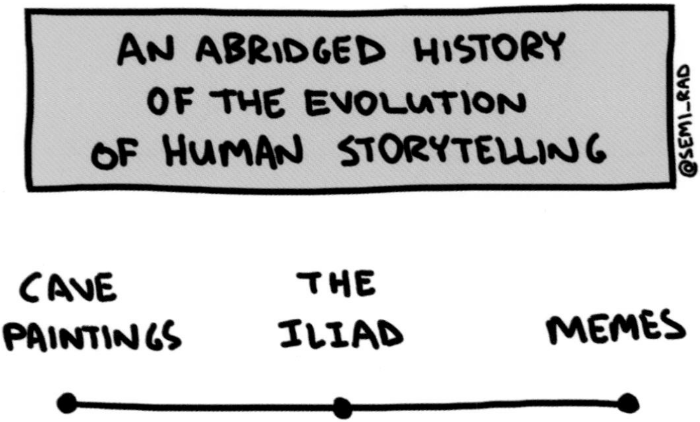
AN ABRIDGED HISTORY OF THE EVOLUTION OF HUMAN STORYTELLING
@SEMI_RAD
CAVE PAINTINGS
THE ILIAD
MEMES

LIFE
ONE WAY TO LOOK AT IT
@SEMI_RAD
PHYSICAL ATTRACTIVENESS/YOUTH
HOW NICE OF AN APARTMENT YOU CAN AFFORD

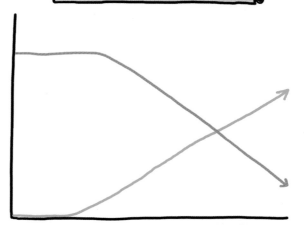

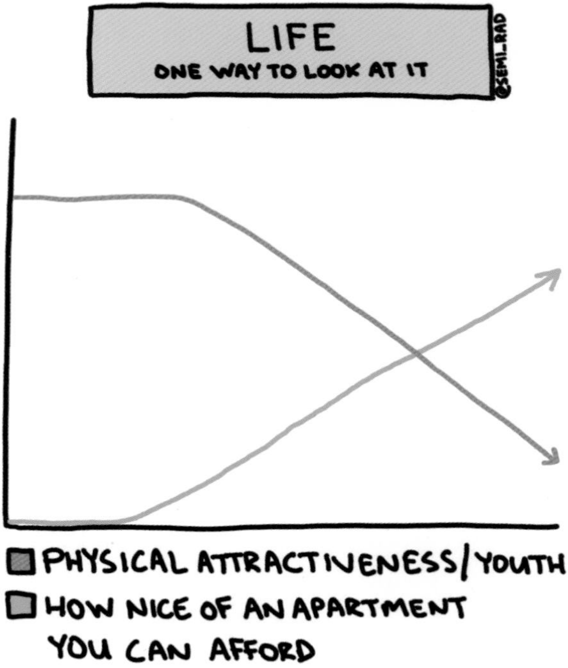

HOW TO REMEMBER TO BUY SOAP FOR THE SHOWER

@SEMI_RAD

DAY 1: WOW, I'M ALMOST OUT OF SOAP

DAY 2: GOTTA REMEMBER TO BUY SOAP

DAY 3: HOPE THIS TINY SHARD OF SOAP LASTS THROUGH THIS SHOWER

DAY 4: (WRITES NOTE TO SELF SAYING "BUY SOAP")

DAY 5: (USES SHAMPOO FOR SOAP)

DAY 6: (E-MAILS SELF: "BUY SOAP")

DAY 10: BUYS SOAP

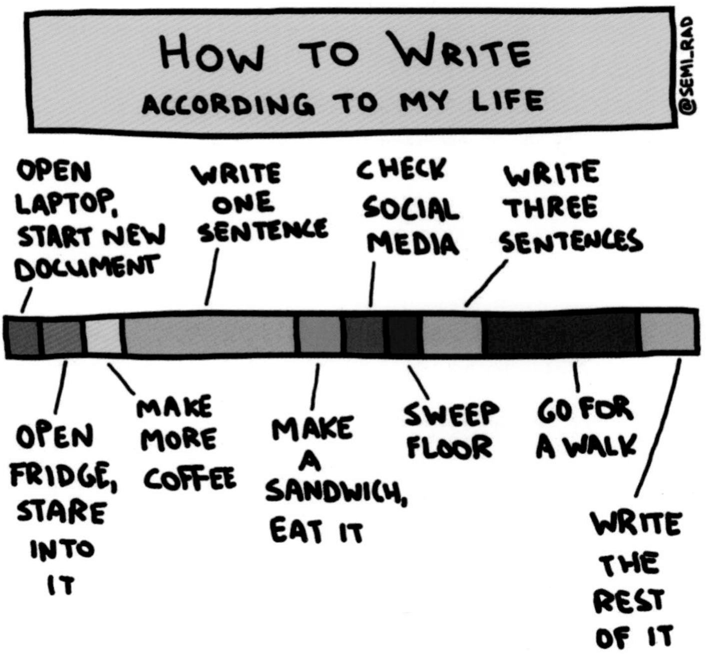

HOW TO WRITE
ACCORDING TO MY LIFE
@SEMI_RAD
OPEN LAPTOP, START NEW DOCUMENT
WRITE ONE SENTENCE
CHECK SOCIAL MEDIA
WRITE THREE SENTENCES
OPEN FRIDGE, STARE INTO IT
MAKE MORE COFFEE
MAKE A SANDWICH, EAT IT
SWEEP FLOOR
GO FOR A WALK
WRITE THE REST OF IT

HOW TO TAKE A COMPLIMENT

ACCORDING TO MY LIFE

@SEMI_RAD

1. LISTEN
2. GROW INCREASINGLY ANXIOUS FOR EVERY .2 SECONDS THE COMPLIMENT LASTS PAST 1.5 SECONDS
3. SAY "THANK YOU"
4. IMMEDIATELY CHANGE THE SUBJECT

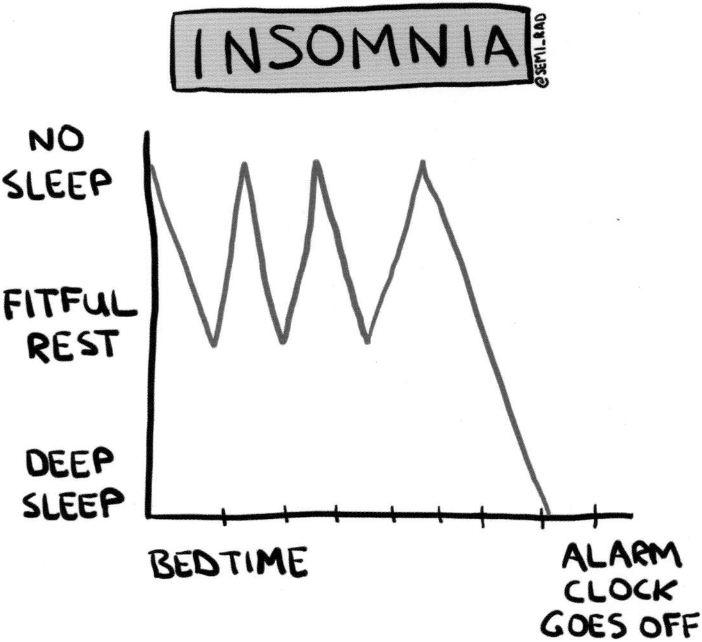
INSOMNIA
@SEMI_RAD
NO SLEEP
FITFUL REST
DEEP SLEEP
BEDTIME
ALARM CLOCK GOES OFF

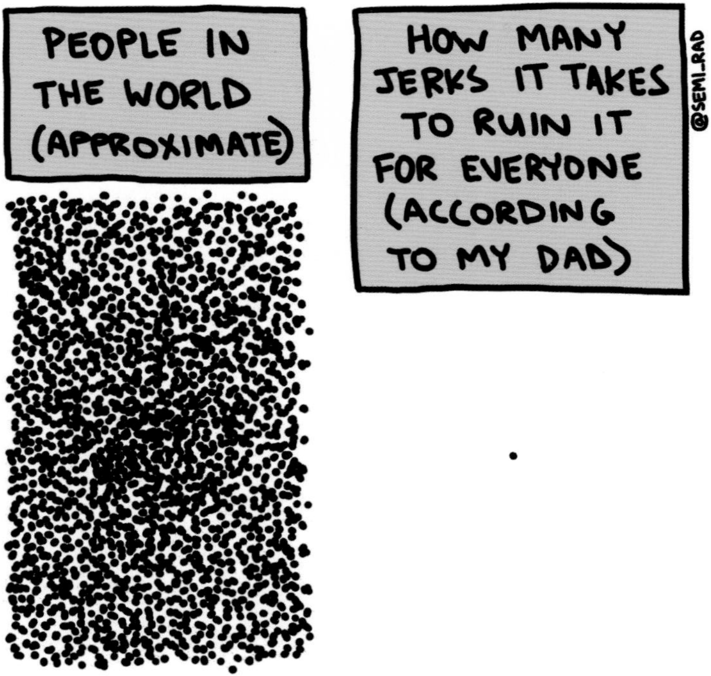
PEOPLE IN THE WORLD (APPROXIMATE)
HOW MANY JERKS IT TAKES TO RUIN IT FOR EVERYONE (ACCORDING TO MY DAD)
@SEMI_RAD

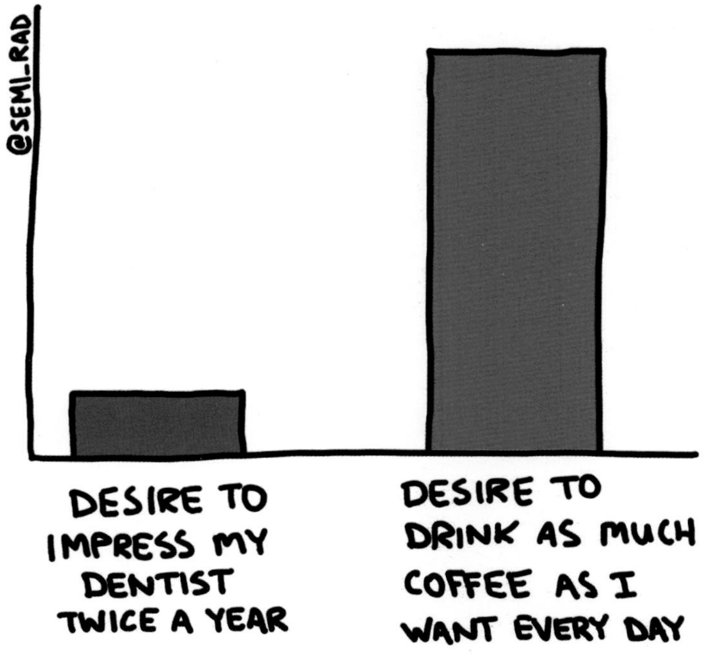
@SEMI_RAD
DESIRE TO IMPRESS MY DENTIST TWICE A YEAR
DESIRE TO DRINK AS MUCH COFFEE AS I WANT EVERY DAY

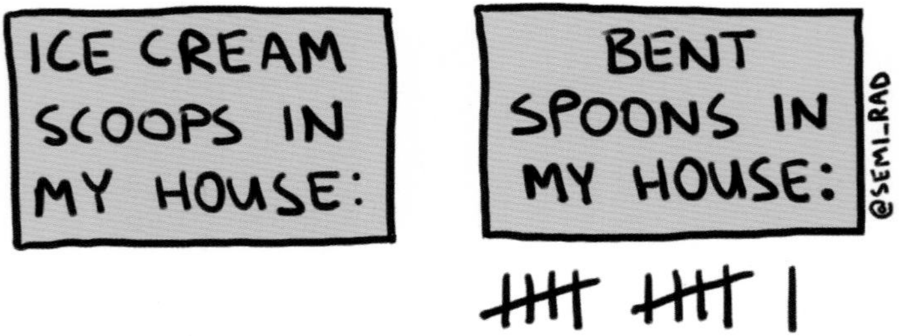
ICE CREAM SCOOPS IN MY HOUSE:
BENT SPOONS IN MY HOUSE:
@SEMI_RAD

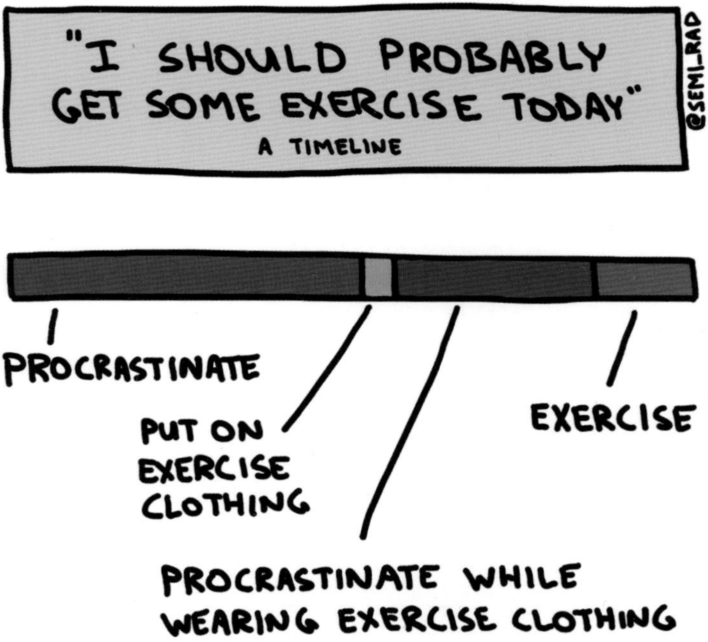
"I SHOULD PROBABLY GET SOME EXERCISE TODAY"
A TIMELINE
@SEMI_RAD
PROCRASTINATE
PUT ON EXERCISE CLOTHING
PROCRASTINATE WHILE WEARING EXERCISE CLOTHING
EXERCISE

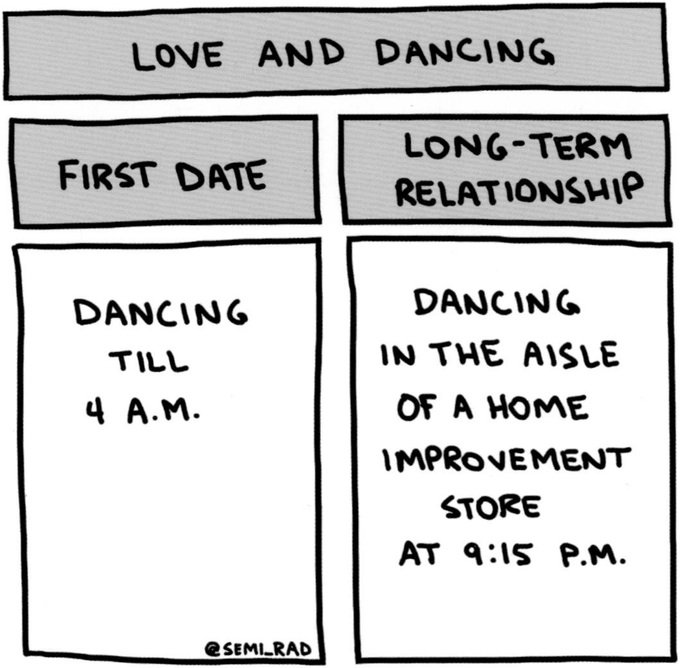
LOVE AND DANCING
FIRST DATE
LONG-TERM RELATIONSHIP
DANCING TILL 4 A.M.
DANCING IN THE AISLE OF A HOME IMPROVEMENT STORE AT 9:15 P.M.
@SEMI_RAD

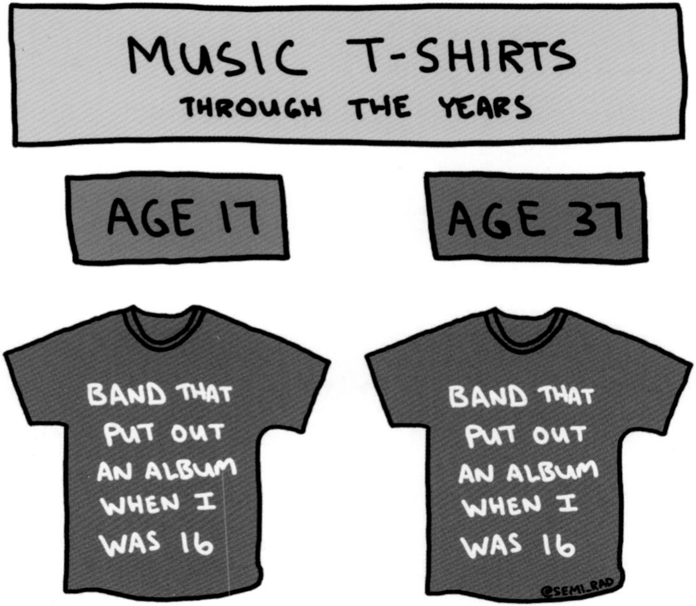
MUSIC T-SHIRTS
THROUGH THE YEARS
AGE 17
AGE 37
BAND THAT PUT OUT AN ALBUM WHEN I WAS 16
BAND THAT PUT OUT AN ALBUM WHEN I WAS 16
@SEMI_RAD

MULTITASKING

9:30 AM I CAN DO THREE THINGS AT ONCE AND GET THEM ALL DONE MUCH MORE QUICKLY!

10:14 AM I HAVE COMPLETED ZERO OF THOSE THREE THINGS BUT I HAVE 4) FOUND A VIDEO OF A DOG RIDING AN ESCALATOR AND 5) SENT IT TO SEVEN PEOPLE

@SEMI_RAD

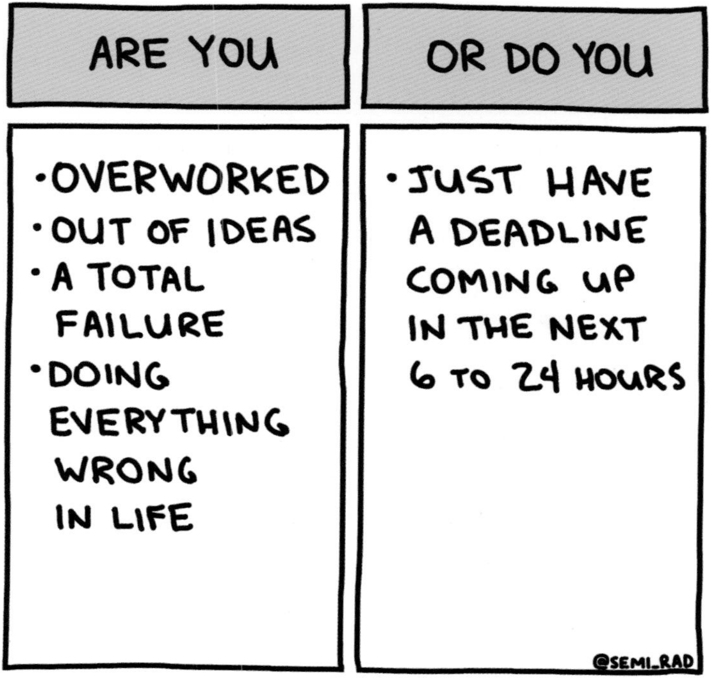
ARE YOU
•OVERWORKED
•OUT OF IDEAS
•A TOTAL FAILURE
•DOING EVERYTHING WRONG IN LIFE
OR DO YOU
•JUST HAVE A DEADLINE COMING UP IN THE NEXT 6 TO 24 HOURS
@SEMI_RAD

NEWTON'S THIRD LAW OF EXERCISE MOTION
@SEMI_RAD
"FOR EVERY ACTION, THERE IS A VERY UNEQUAL AND OPPOSITE REACTION"
CALORIES
+
−
(RUNS MORE THAN 2 MILES)
(EATS ENTIRE PIZZA)
(AND SOME ICE CREAM)

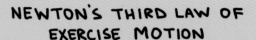

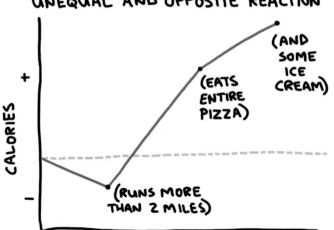

LOVE AND TALKING
NEW RELATIONSHIP
LONG-TERM RELATIONSHIP
"I FEEL LIKE I COULD JUST TALK TO YOU ALL NIGHT"
@SEMI_RAD
I WILL ATTEMPT TO TALK TO YOU WHEN YOU ARE IN THE NEXT ROOM AND CAN'T REALLY HEAR ME

NEGATIVITY

@SEMI_RAD

"THIS SIDEWALK IS COMPLETELY COVERED IN DOG SHIT"

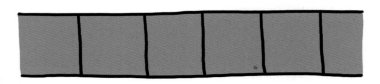

□ = SIDEWALK

■ = DOG SHIT

WHO'S A GOOD BOY?
THE MALE DOG CURRENTLY BEING QUESTIONED
@SEMI_RAD

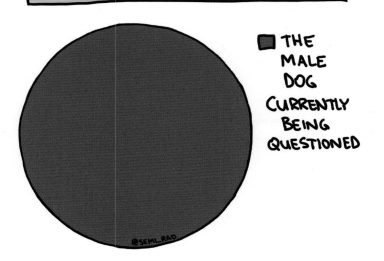

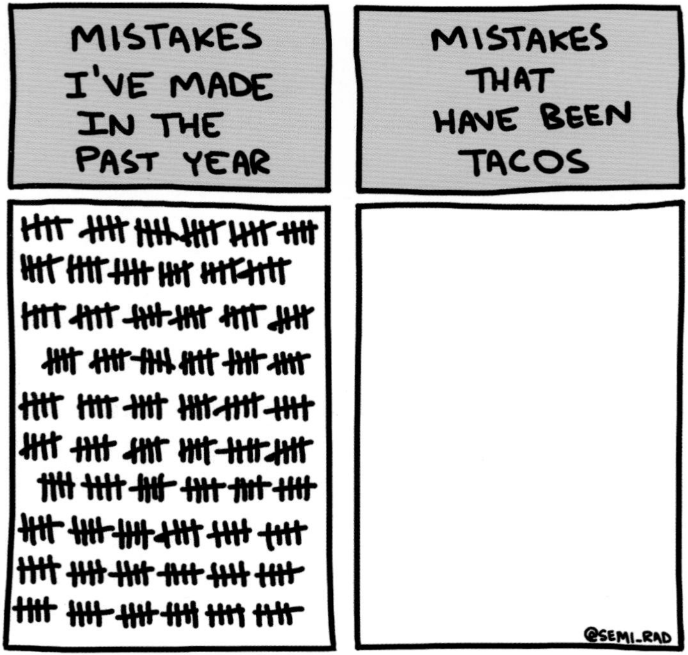
MISTAKES I'VE MADE IN THE PAST YEAR
MISTAKES THAT HAVE BEEN TACOS
@SEMI_RAD

HOW TO GET A HAIRCUT
ACCORDING TO MY LIFE

@SEMI_RAD

1. LOOK IN THE MIRROR AND SAY, "I NEED A HAIRCUT"
2. REPEAT STEP 1 2 TO 300 TIMES OVER DAYS OR WEEKS
3. GET A HAIRCUT
4. LOOK IN THE MIRROR AND SAY, "I'VE MADE A TERRIBLE MISTAKE"
5. REPEAT STEPS 1-4 UNTIL DEATH

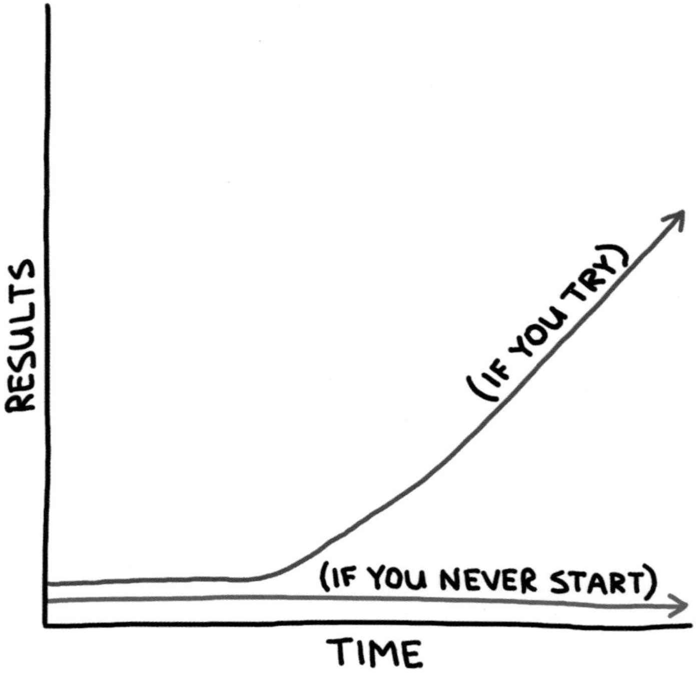
RESULTS
(IF YOU TRY)
(IF YOU NEVER START)
TIME

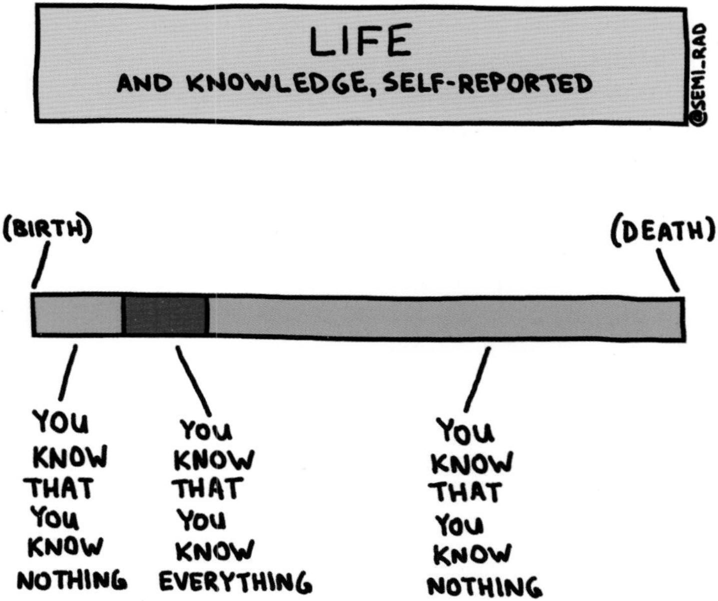
LIFE
AND KNOWLEDGE, SELF-REPORTED
@SEMI_RAD
(BIRTH)
(DEATH)
YOU KNOW THAT YOU KNOW NOTHING
YOU KNOW THAT YOU KNOW EVERYTHING
YOU KNOW THAT YOU KNOW NOTHING

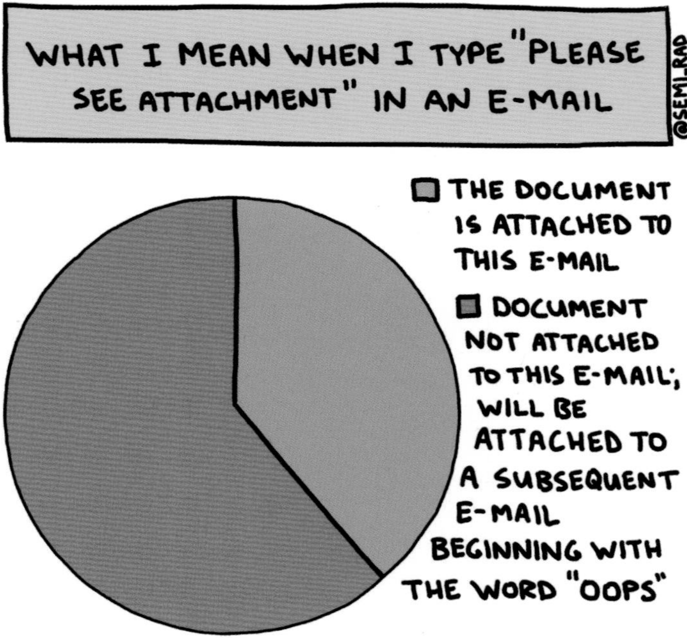
WHAT I MEAN WHEN I TYPE "PLEASE SEE ATTACHMENT" IN AN E-MAIL
@SEMI_RAD
THE DOCUMENT IS ATTACHED TO THIS E-MAIL
DOCUMENT NOT ATTACHED TO THIS E-MAIL; WILL BE ATTACHED TO A SUBSEQUENT E-MAIL BEGINNING WITH THE WORD "OOPS"

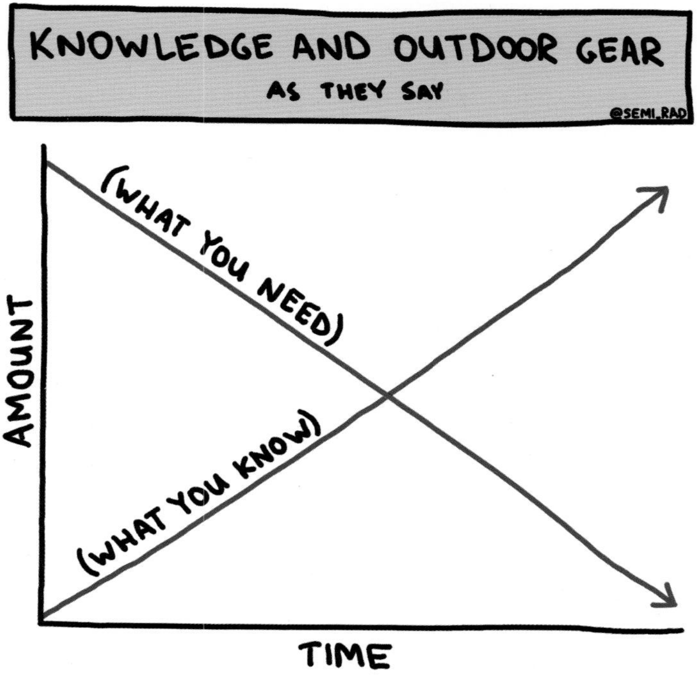
KNOWLEDGE AND OUTDOOR GEAR
AS THEY SAY
@SEMI_RAD
(WHAT YOU NEED)
(WHAT YOU KNOW)
AMOUNT
TIME

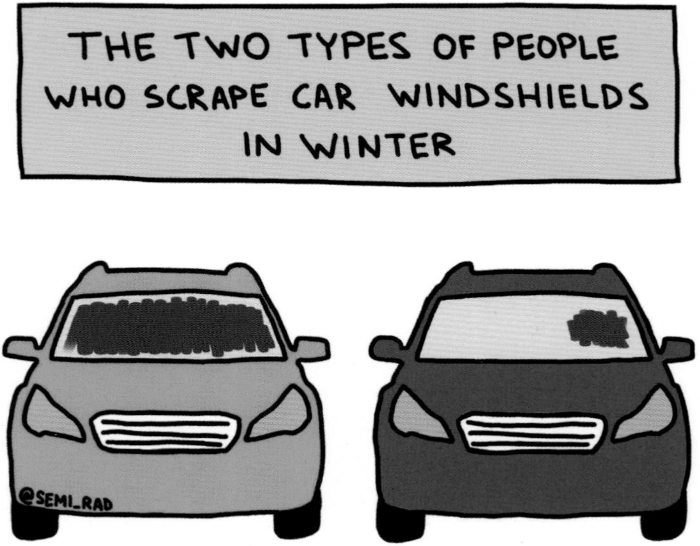
THE TWO TYPES OF PEOPLE WHO SCRAPE CAR WINDSHIELDS IN WINTER
@SEMI_RAD

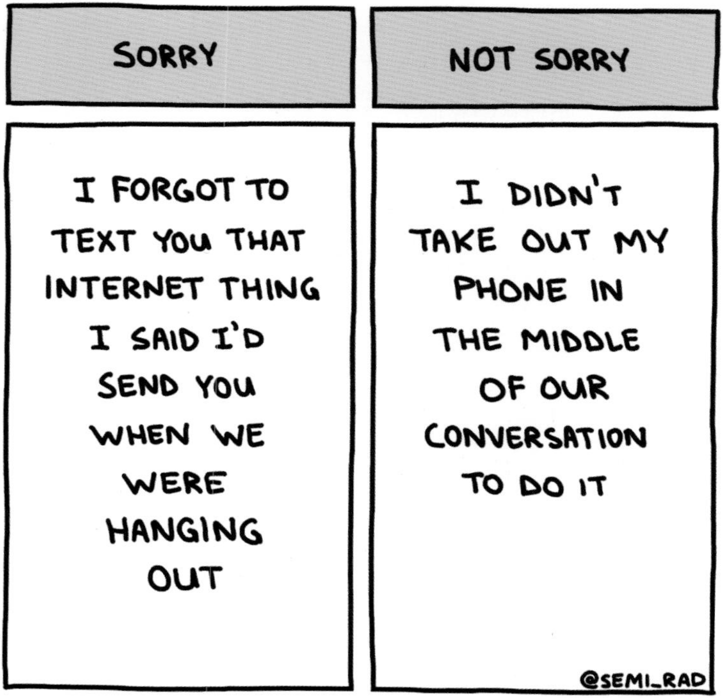
SORRY
NOT SORRY
I FORGOT TO TEXT YOU THAT INTERNET THING I SAID I'D SEND YOU WHEN WE WERE HANGING OUT
I DIDN'T TAKE OUT MY PHONE IN THE MIDDLE OF OUR CONVERSATION TO DO IT
@SEMI_RAD

WHAT ARE WE RUNNING FROM?

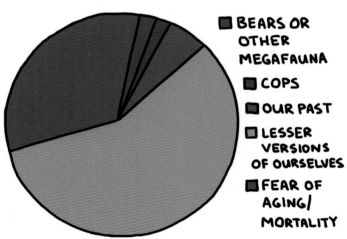

- BEARS OR OTHER MEGAFAUNA
- COPS
- OUR PAST
- LESSER VERSIONS OF OURSELVES
- FEAR OF AGING/ MORTALITY

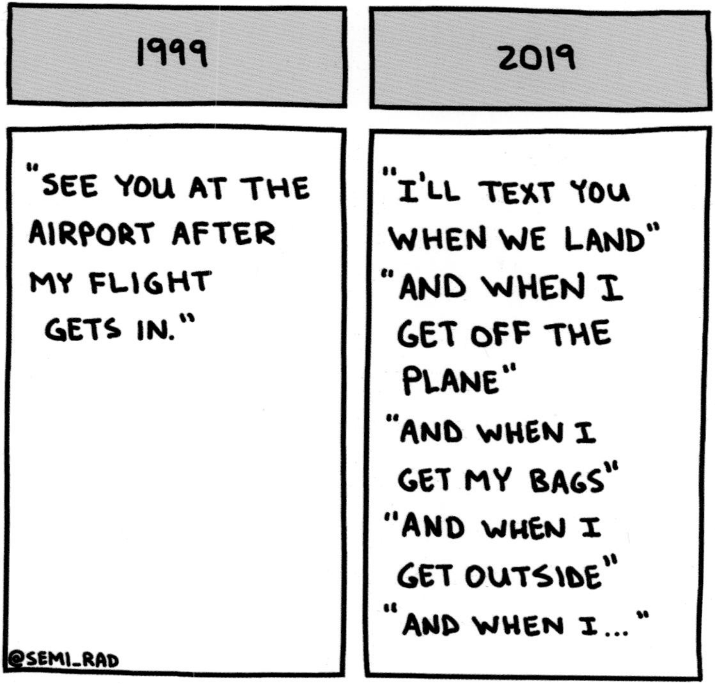
1999
2019
"SEE YOU AT THE AIRPORT AFTER MY FLIGHT GETS IN."
@SEMI_RAD
"I'LL TEXT YOU WHEN WE LAND"
"AND WHEN I GET OFF THE PLANE"
"AND WHEN I GET MY BAGS"
"AND WHEN I GET OUTSIDE"
"AND WHEN I..."

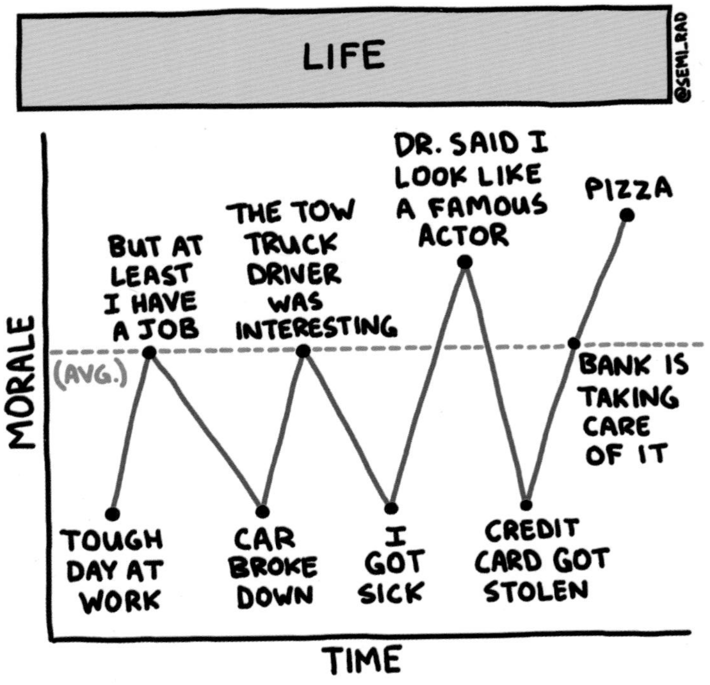
LIFE
@SEMI_RAD
MORALE
(AVG.)
TIME
TOUGH DAY AT WORK
BUT AT LEAST I HAVE A JOB
CAR BROKE DOWN
THE TOW TRUCK DRIVER WAS INTERESTING
I GOT SICK
DR. SAID I LOOK LIKE A FAMOUS ACTOR
CREDIT CARD GOT STOLEN
BANK IS TAKING CARE OF IT
PIZZA

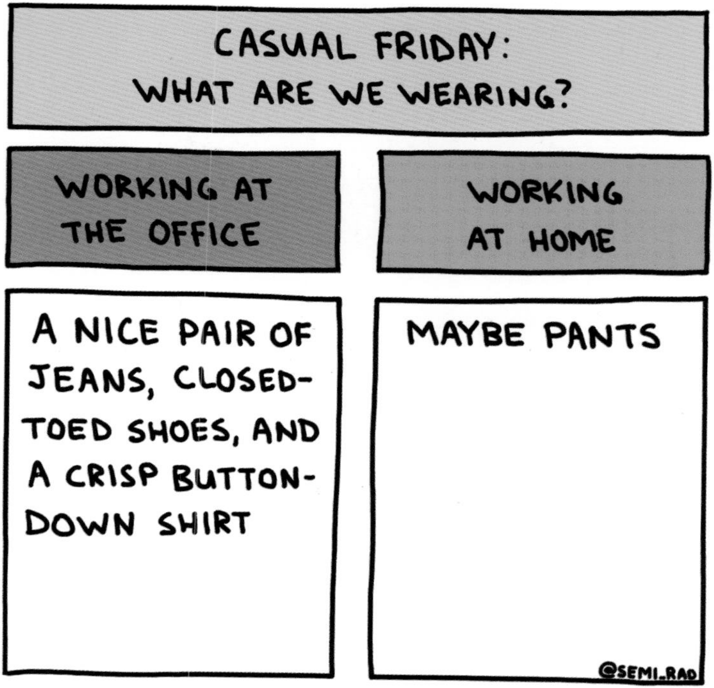
CASUAL FRIDAY:
WHAT ARE WE WEARING?
WORKING AT THE OFFICE
WORKING AT HOME
A NICE PAIR OF JEANS, CLOSED-TOED SHOES, AND A CRISP BUTTON-DOWN SHIRT
MAYBE PANTS
@SEMI_RAD

MORNING
A TIMELINE
@SEMI_RAD
SLEEP
DON'T EVEN FUCKING TALK TO ME
COFFEE
LUNCH

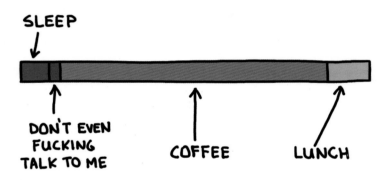

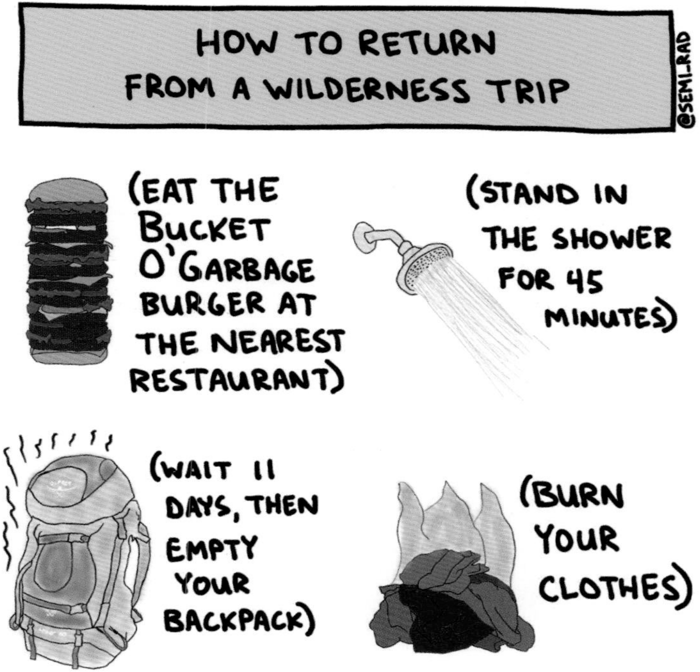
HOW TO RETURN FROM A WILDERNESS TRIP
@SEMI_RAD
(EAT THE BUCKET O'GARBAGE BURGER AT THE NEAREST RESTAURANT)
(STAND IN THE SHOWER FOR 45 MINUTES)
(WAIT 11 DAYS, THEN EMPTY YOUR BACKPACK)
(BURN YOUR CLOTHES)

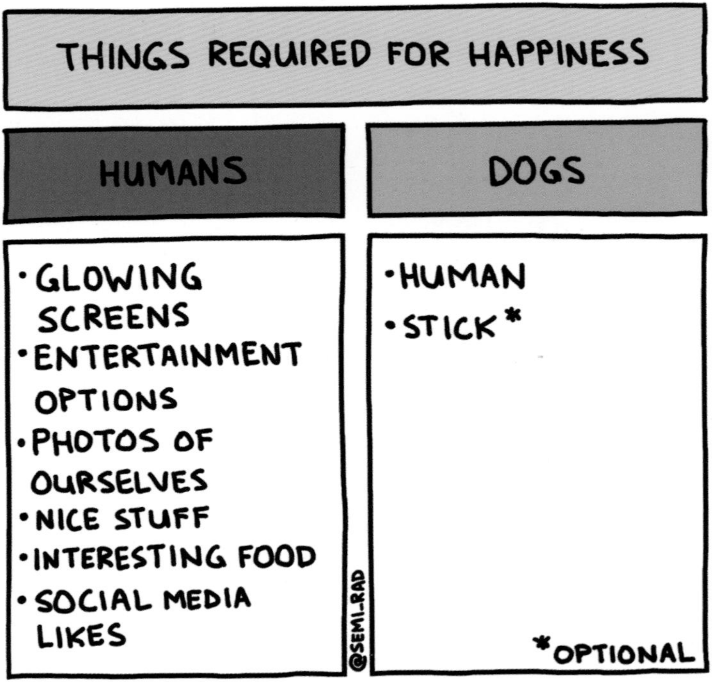
THINGS REQUIRED FOR HAPPINESS
HUMANS
DOGS
• GLOWING SCREENS
• ENTERTAINMENT OPTIONS
• PHOTOS OF OURSELVES
• NICE STUFF
• INTERESTING FOOD
• SOCIAL MEDIA LIKES
• HUMAN
• STICK*
*OPTIONAL
@SEMI-RAD

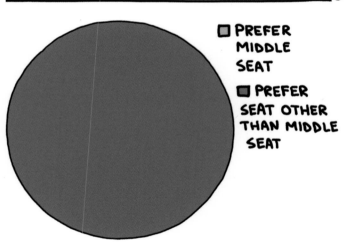

PERCENTAGE OF PEOPLE WHO PREFER
MIDDLE SEATS ON AIRPLANES,
ACCORDING TO MY FRIEND SYD JONES

@SEMI_RAD

□ PREFER
MIDDLE
SEAT

□ PREFER
SEAT OTHER
THAN MIDDLE
SEAT

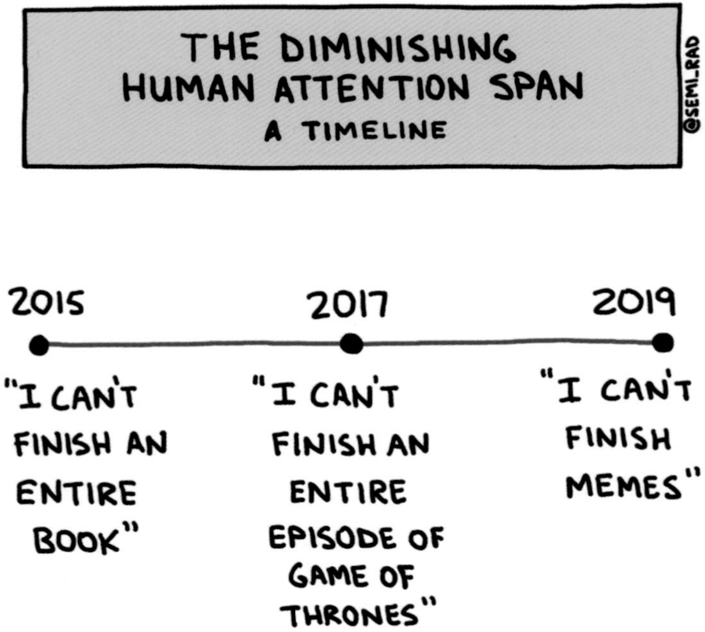
THE DIMINISHING
HUMAN ATTENTION SPAN
A TIMELINE
@SEMI_RAD
2015
2017
2019
"I CAN'T FINISH AN ENTIRE BOOK"
"I CAN'T FINISH AN ENTIRE EPISODE OF GAME OF THRONES"
"I CAN'T FINISH MEMES"

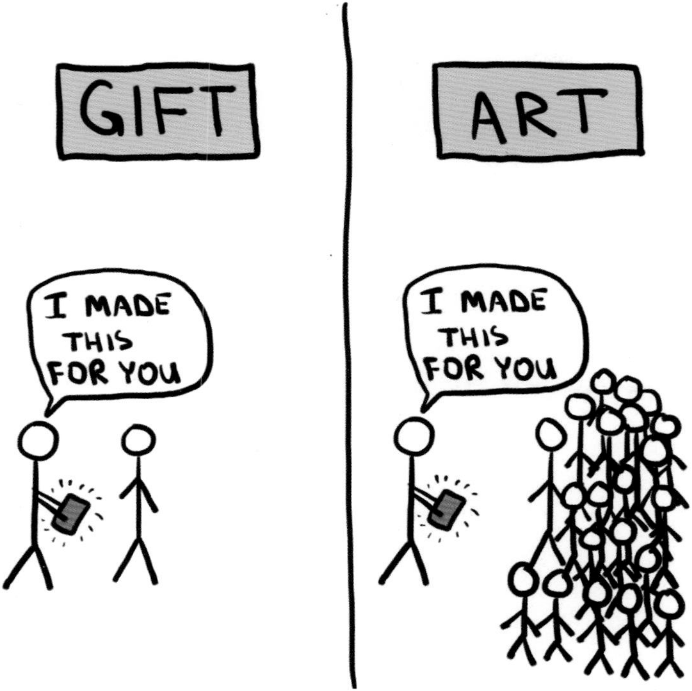
GIFT
I MADE THIS FOR YOU
ART
I MADE THIS FOR YOU

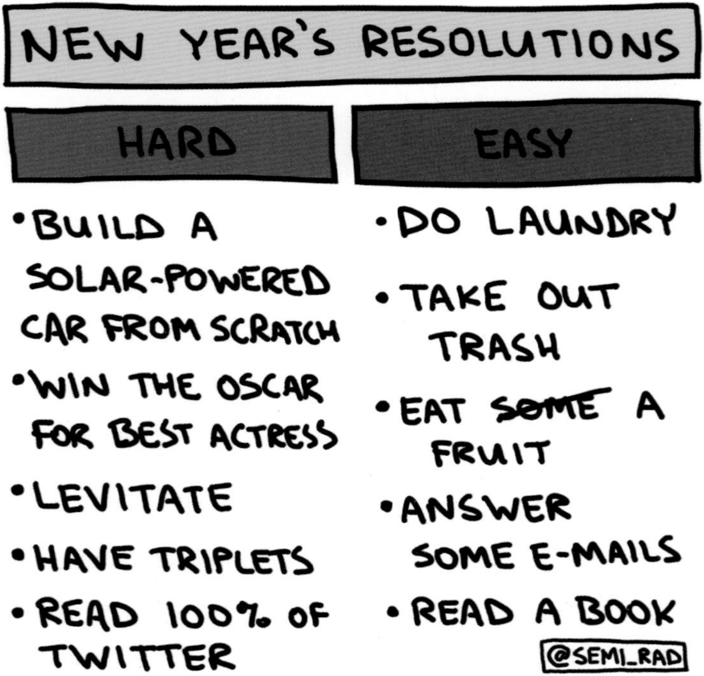
NEW YEAR'S RESOLUTIONS
HARD
EASY
• BUILD A SOLAR-POWERED CAR FROM SCRATCH
• WIN THE OSCAR FOR BEST ACTRESS
• LEVITATE
• HAVE TRIPLETS
• READ 100% OF TWITTER
• DO LAUNDRY
• TAKE OUT TRASH
• EAT ~~SOME~~ A FRUIT
• ANSWER SOME E-MAILS
• READ A BOOK
@SEMI_RAD

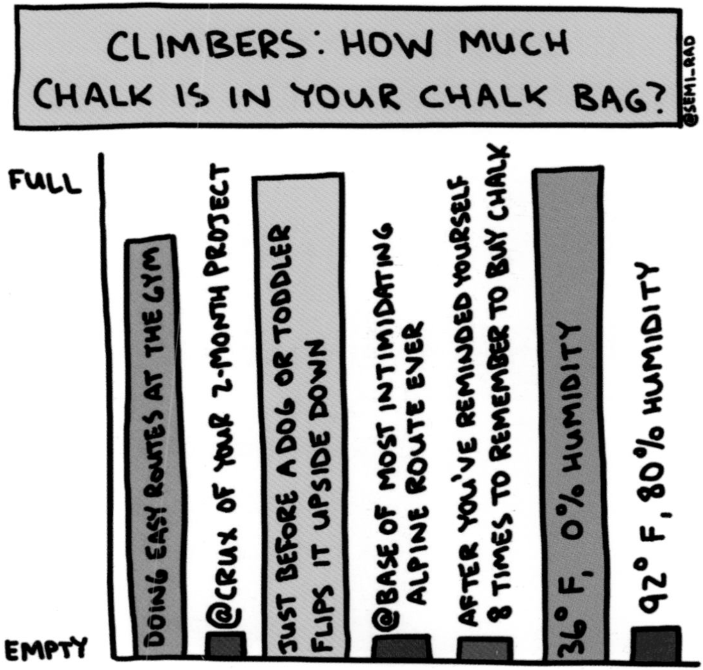
CLIMBERS: HOW MUCH CHALK IS IN YOUR CHALK BAG?
@SEMI_RAD
FULL
EMPTY
DOING EASY ROUTES AT THE GYM
@CRUX OF YOUR 2-MONTH PROJECT
JUST BEFORE A DOG OR TODDLER FLIPS IT UPSIDE DOWN
@BASE OF MOST INTIMIDATING ALPINE ROUTE EVER
AFTER YOU'VE REMINDED YOURSELF 8 TIMES TO REMEMBER TO BUY CHALK
36° F, 0% HUMIDITY
92° F, 80% HUMIDITY

HOW TO SPELL SOMEONE'S NAME CORRECTLY WHEN ADDRESSING THEM IN AN EMAIL

@SEMI_RAD

STEP 1 GIVE A SHIT

STEP 2 CHECK THEIR EMAIL ADDRESS OR THEIR SIGNATURE FROM THEIR LAST EMAIL TO YOU FOR CLUES ABOUT THE CORRECT SPELLING OF THEIR NAME

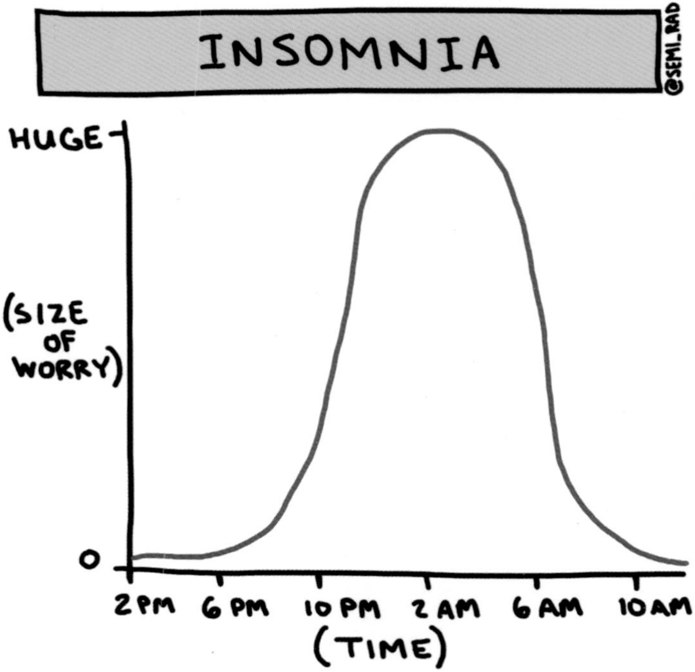
INSOMNIA
@SEMI_RAD
HUGE
(SIZE OF WORRY)
0
2PM
6 PM
10 PM
2 AM
6 AM
10AM
(TIME)

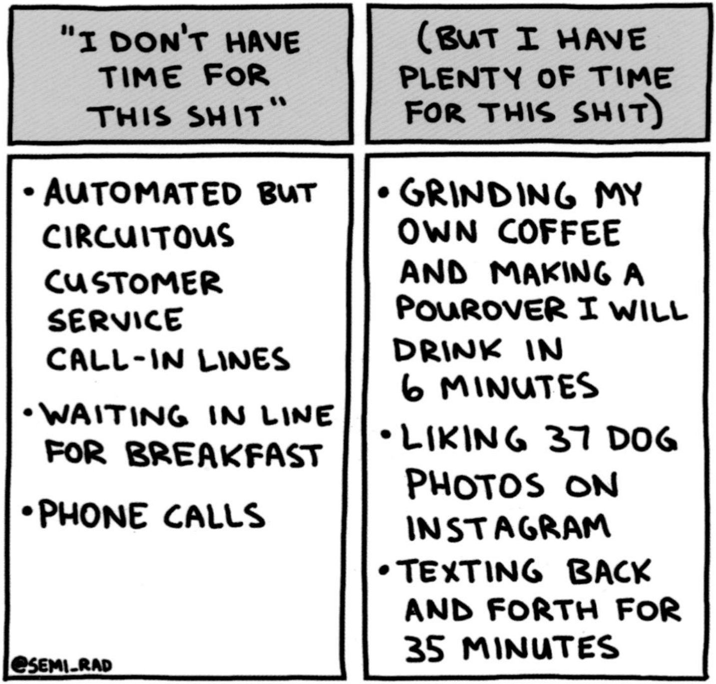
"I DON'T HAVE TIME FOR THIS SHIT"
(BUT I HAVE PLENTY OF TIME FOR THIS SHIT)
• AUTOMATED BUT CIRCUITOUS CUSTOMER SERVICE CALL-IN LINES
• WAITING IN LINE FOR BREAKFAST
• PHONE CALLS
@SEMI_RAD
• GRINDING MY OWN COFFEE AND MAKING A POUROVER I WILL DRINK IN 6 MINUTES
• LIKING 37 DOG PHOTOS ON INSTAGRAM
• TEXTING BACK AND FORTH FOR 35 MINUTES

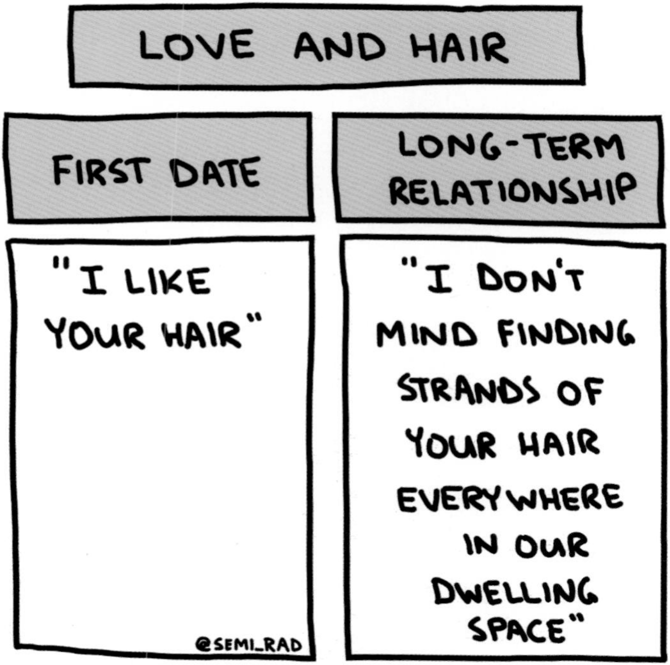
LOVE AND HAIR
FIRST DATE
LONG-TERM RELATIONSHIP
"I LIKE YOUR HAIR"
@SEMI_RAD
"I DON'T MIND FINDING STRANDS OF YOUR HAIR EVERYWHERE IN OUR DWELLING SPACE"

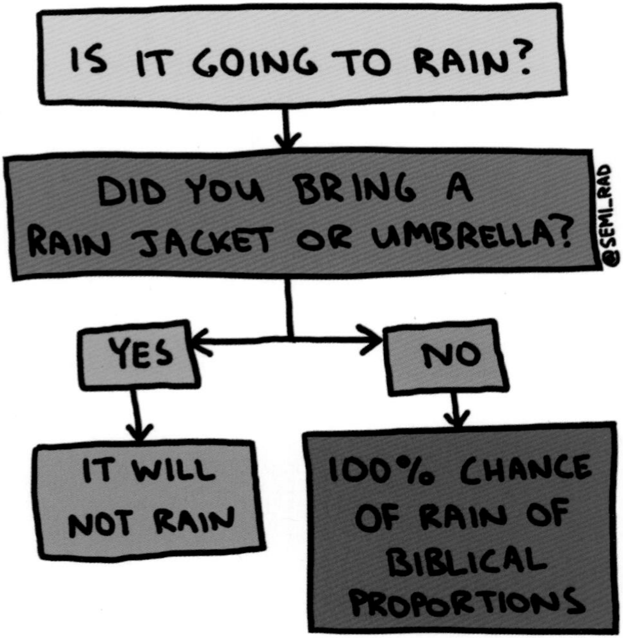

IS IT GOING TO RAIN?
DID YOU BRING A RAIN JACKET OR UMBRELLA?
@SEMI_RAD
YES
NO
IT WILL NOT RAIN
100% CHANCE OF RAIN OF BIBLICAL PROPORTIONS

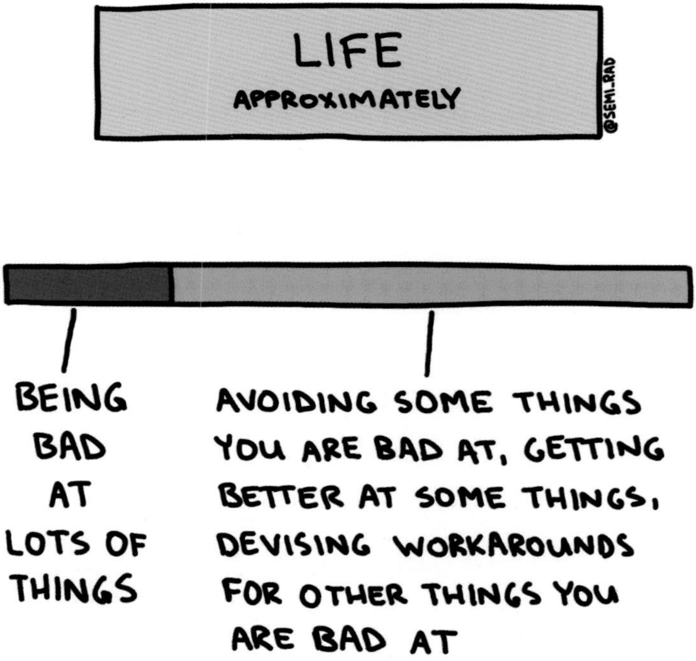
LIFE
APPROXIMATELY
@SEMI_RAD
BEING BAD AT LOTS OF THINGS
AVOIDING SOME THINGS YOU ARE BAD AT, GETTING BETTER AT SOME THINGS, DEVISING WORKAROUNDS FOR OTHER THINGS YOU ARE BAD AT

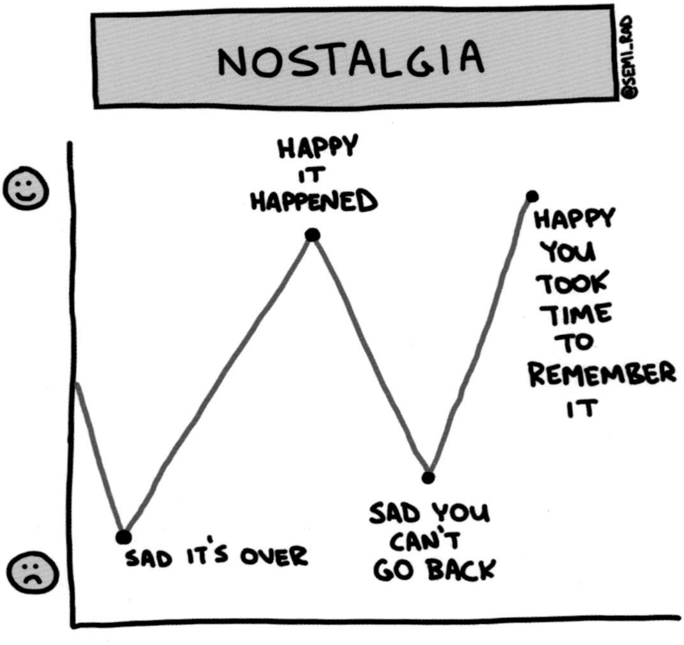
NOSTALGIA
@SEMI_RAD
HAPPY IT HAPPENED
HAPPY YOU TOOK TIME TO REMEMBER IT
SAD IT'S OVER
SAD YOU CAN'T GO BACK

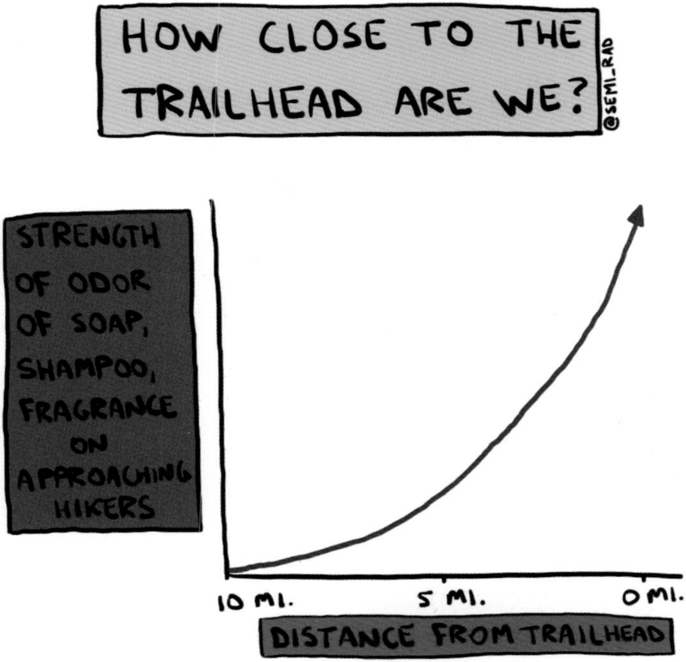
HOW CLOSE TO THE TRAILHEAD ARE WE?
@SEMI_RAD
STRENGTH OF ODOR OF SOAP, SHAMPOO, FRAGRANCE ON APPROACHING HIKERS
10 MI.
5 MI.
0 MI.
DISTANCE FROM TRAILHEAD

TIPS FOR INCREASING ANXIETY

@SEMI_RAD

- COMMIT TO EVERYTHING
- TRY TO PLEASE EVERYONE
- THINK ABOUT RATIONAL + IRRATIONAL "WHAT IFs"
- LOOK AT MORE GLOWING SCREENS
- THINK ABOUT RATIONAL + IRRATIONAL "WHAT IFs" IN BED
- + MORE COFFEE

SKIN: A COMEDY, A TRAGEDY
@SEMI_RAD
ZITS
YOUR 30s
WRINKLES

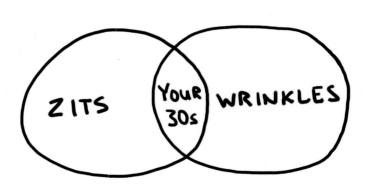

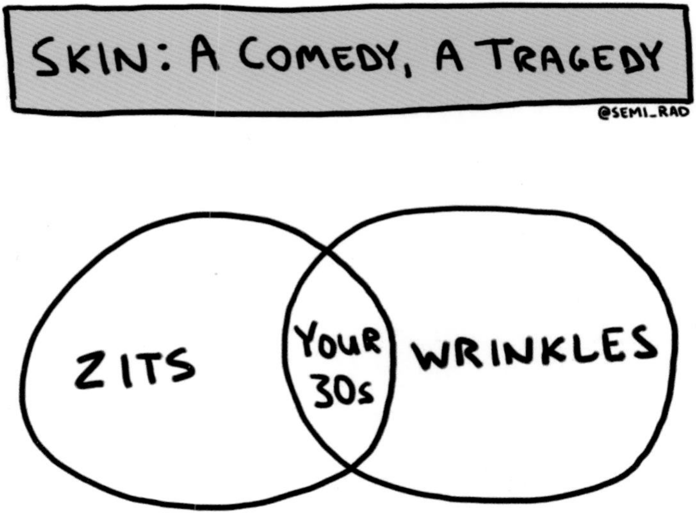

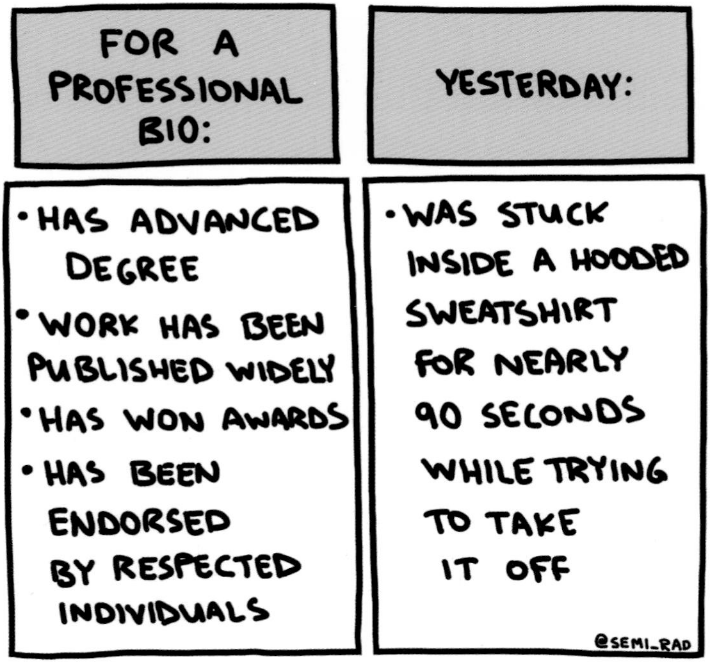
FOR A PROFESSIONAL BIO:
YESTERDAY:
• HAS ADVANCED DEGREE
• WORK HAS BEEN PUBLISHED WIDELY
• HAS WON AWARDS
• HAS BEEN ENDORSED BY RESPECTED INDIVIDUALS
• WAS STUCK INSIDE A HOODED SWEATSHIRT FOR NEARLY 90 SECONDS WHILE TRYING TO TAKE IT OFF
@SEMI_RAD

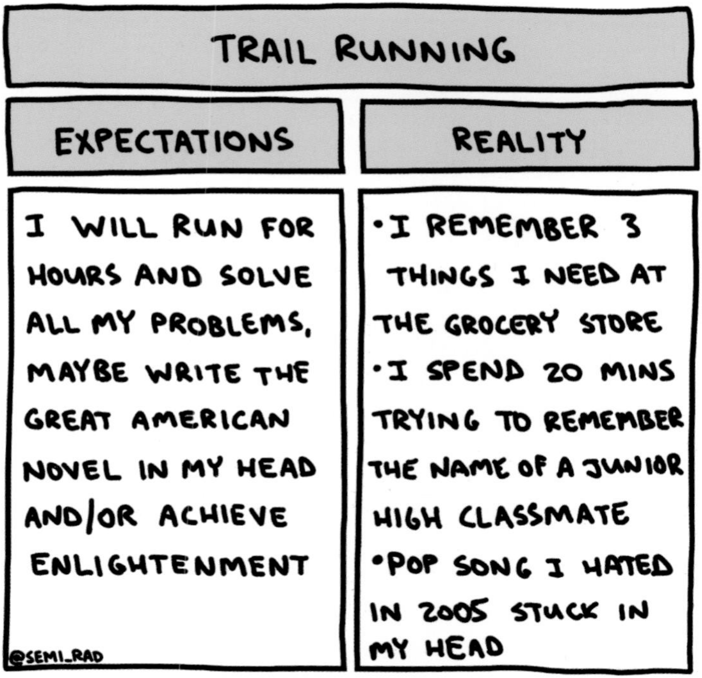
TRAIL RUNNING
EXPECTATIONS
REALITY
I WILL RUN FOR HOURS AND SOLVE ALL MY PROBLEMS, MAYBE WRITE THE GREAT AMERICAN NOVEL IN MY HEAD AND/OR ACHIEVE ENLIGHTENMENT
• I REMEMBER 3 THINGS I NEED AT THE GROCERY STORE
• I SPEND 20 MINS TRYING TO REMEMBER THE NAME OF A JUNIOR HIGH CLASSMATE
• POP SONG I HATED IN 2005 STUCK IN MY HEAD
@SEMI_RAD

THE FIRST SIGNS OF WINTER

@SEMI_RAD

- THE CHILL IN THE AIR
- THE WARM GLOW OF HOLIDAY LIGHTS
- THE FIRST SNOW BLANKETING THE NEIGHBORHOOD
- GUY WALKING AROUND IN A T-SHIRT, INSISTING IT'S NOT THAT COLD

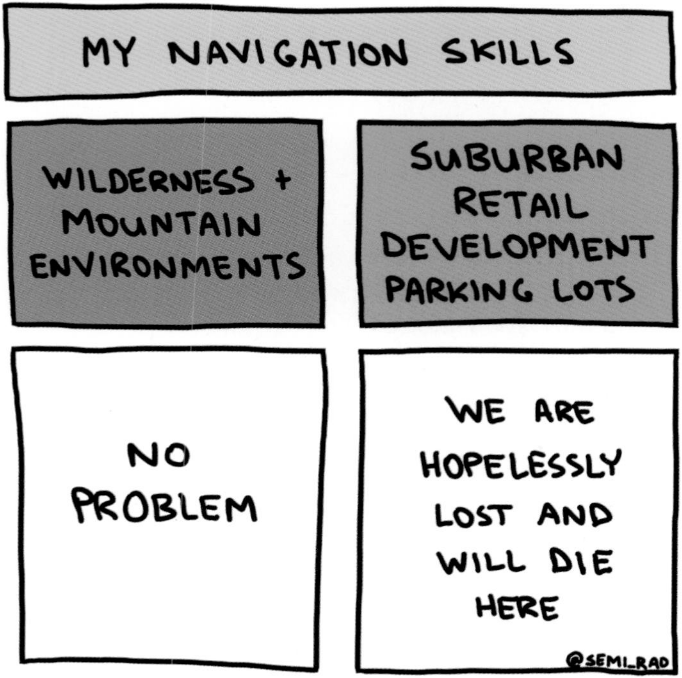
MY NAVIGATION SKILLS
WILDERNESS + MOUNTAIN ENVIRONMENTS
SUBURBAN RETAIL DEVELOPMENT PARKING LOTS
NO PROBLEM
WE ARE HOPELESSLY LOST AND WILL DIE HERE
@SEMI_RAD

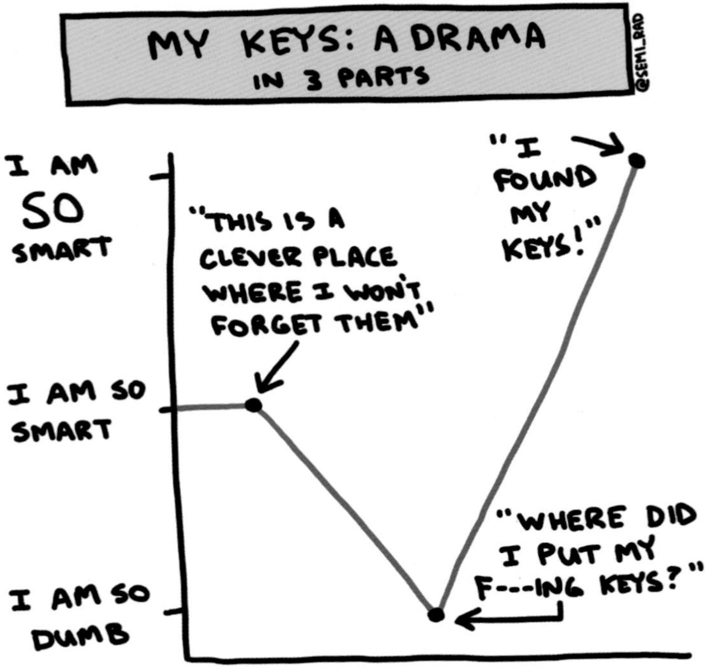
MY KEYS: A DRAMA
IN 3 PARTS
@SEMI_RAD
I AM SO SMART
I AM SO SMART
I AM SO DUMB
"THIS IS A CLEVER PLACE WHERE I WON'T FORGET THEM"
"WHERE DID I PUT MY F---ING KEYS?"
"I FOUND MY KEYS!"

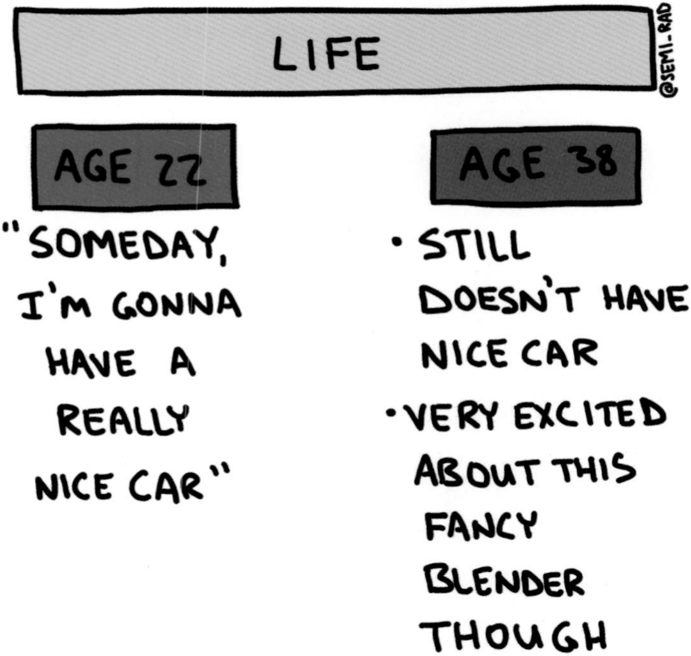
LIFE
@SEMI_RAD
AGE 22
"SOMEDAY, I'M GONNA HAVE A REALLY NICE CAR"
AGE 38
• STILL DOESN'T HAVE NICE CAR
• VERY EXCITED ABOUT THIS FANCY BLENDER THOUGH

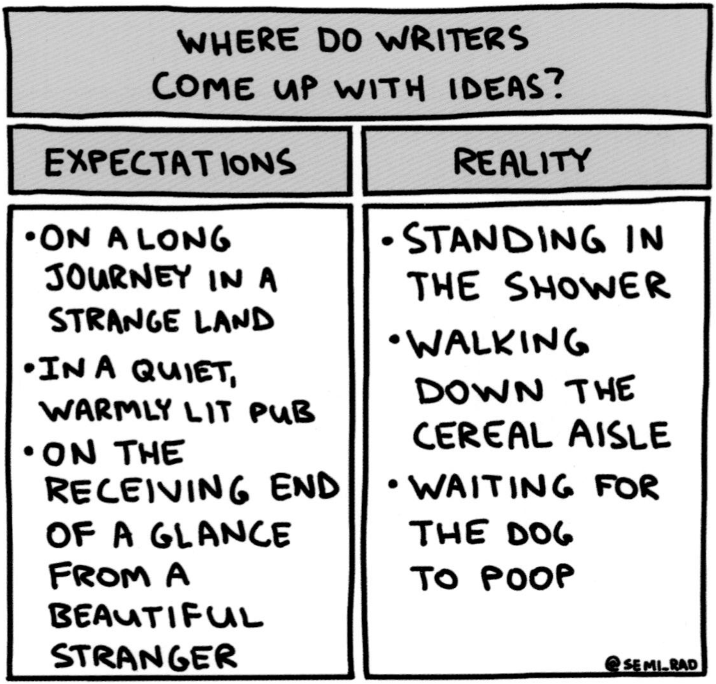
WHERE DO WRITERS COME UP WITH IDEAS?
EXPECTATIONS
REALITY
•ON A LONG JOURNEY IN A STRANGE LAND
•IN A QUIET, WARMLY LIT PUB
•ON THE RECEIVING END OF A GLANCE FROM A BEAUTIFUL STRANGER
•STANDING IN THE SHOWER
•WALKING DOWN THE CEREAL AISLE
•WAITING FOR THE DOG TO POOP
@SEMI_RAD

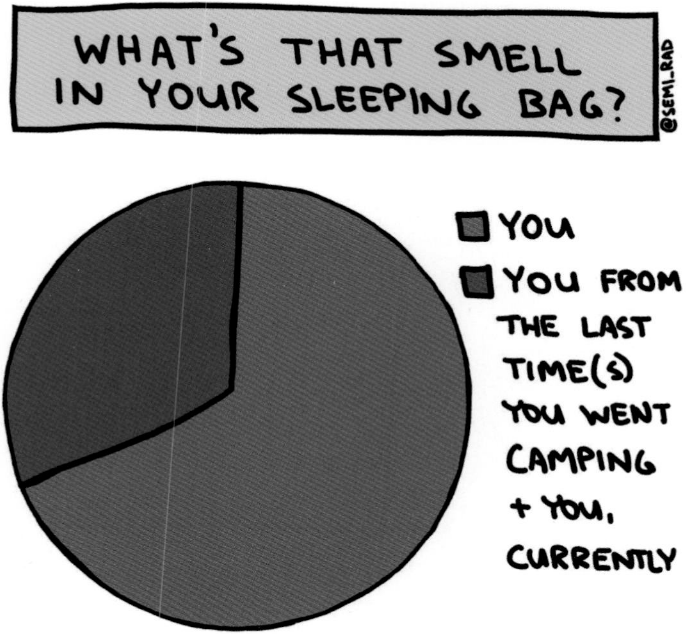
WHAT'S THAT SMELL IN YOUR SLEEPING BAG?
@SEMI_RAD
YOU
YOU FROM THE LAST TIME(S) YOU WENT CAMPING + YOU, CURRENTLY

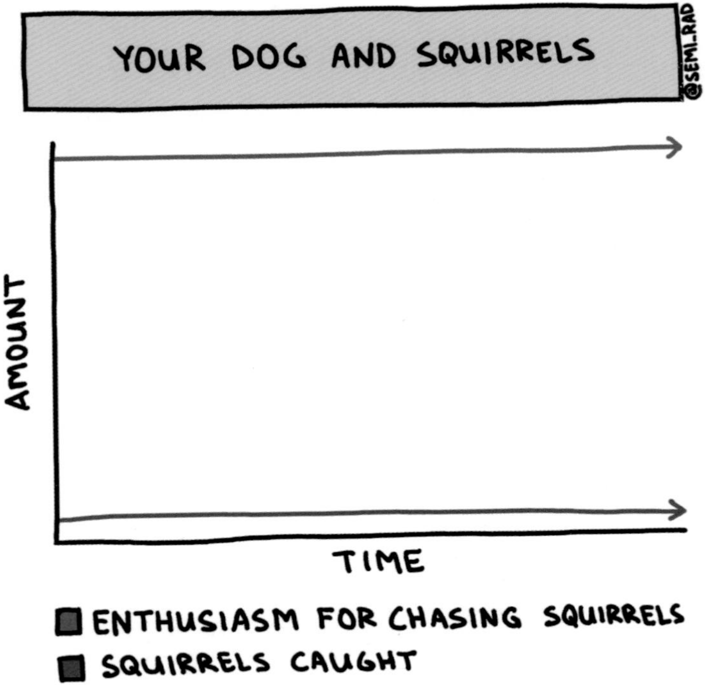
YOUR DOG AND SQUIRRELS
@SEMI_RAD
AMOUNT
TIME
ENTHUSIASM FOR CHASING SQUIRRELS
SQUIRRELS CAUGHT

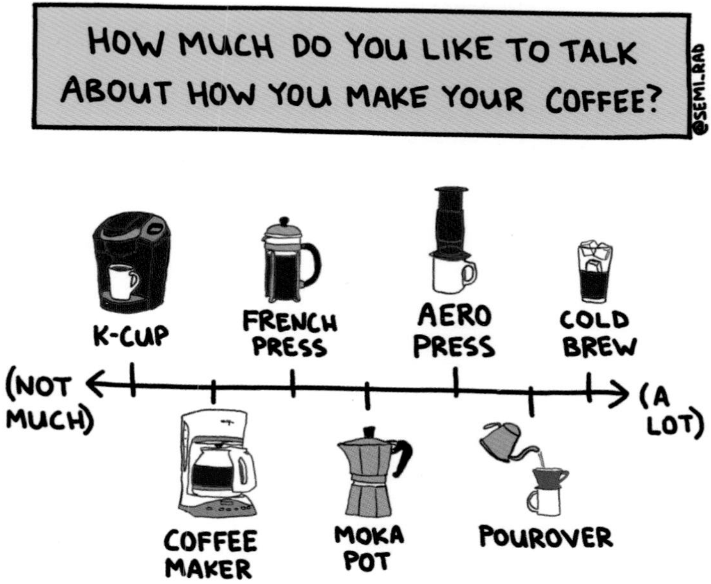
HOW MUCH DO YOU LIKE TO TALK ABOUT HOW YOU MAKE YOUR COFFEE?
@SEMI_RAD
K-CUP
FRENCH PRESS
AERO PRESS
COLD BREW
(NOT MUCH)
(A LOT)
COFFEE MAKER
MOKA POT
POUROVER

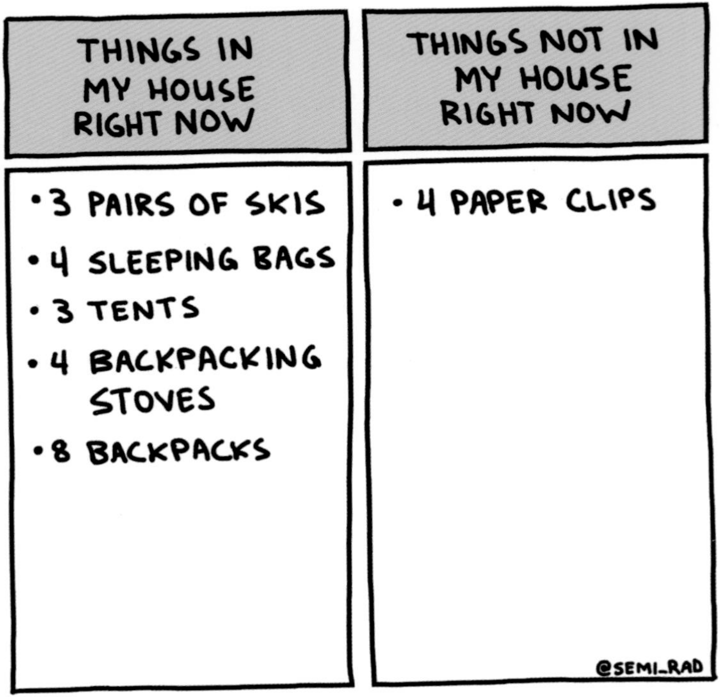
THINGS IN MY HOUSE RIGHT NOW
THINGS NOT IN MY HOUSE RIGHT NOW
• 3 PAIRS OF SKIS
• 4 SLEEPING BAGS
• 3 TENTS
• 4 BACKPACKING STOVES
• 8 BACKPACKS
• 4 PAPER CLIPS
@SEMI_RAD

OKAYNESS OF BODY PARTS HITTING THE GROUND WHILE TRAIL RUNNING

@SEMI_RAD

◼ = GENERALLY OK

◼ = GENERALLY UNDESIRABLE BUT SOMETIMES OK

◼ = GENERALLY NOT OK AT ALL

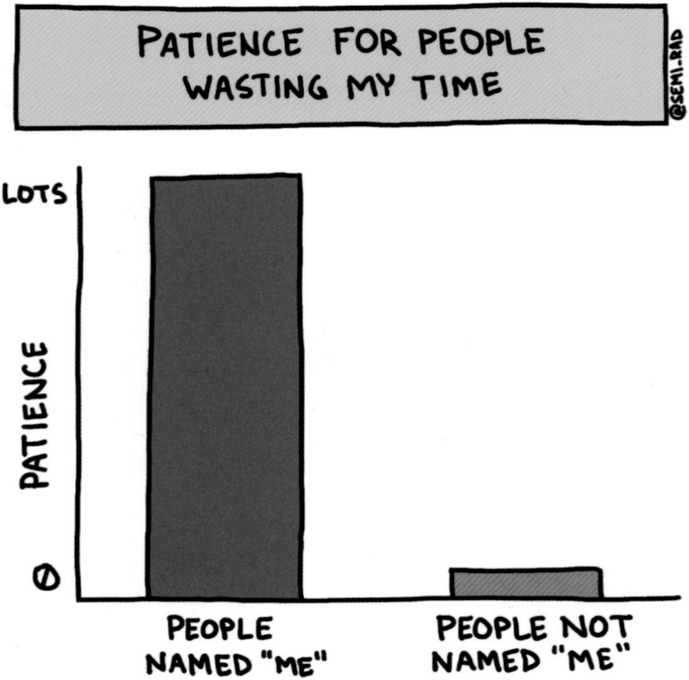
PATIENCE FOR PEOPLE WASTING MY TIME
@SEMI_RAD
LOTS
PATIENCE
0
PEOPLE NAMED "ME"
PEOPLE NOT NAMED "ME"

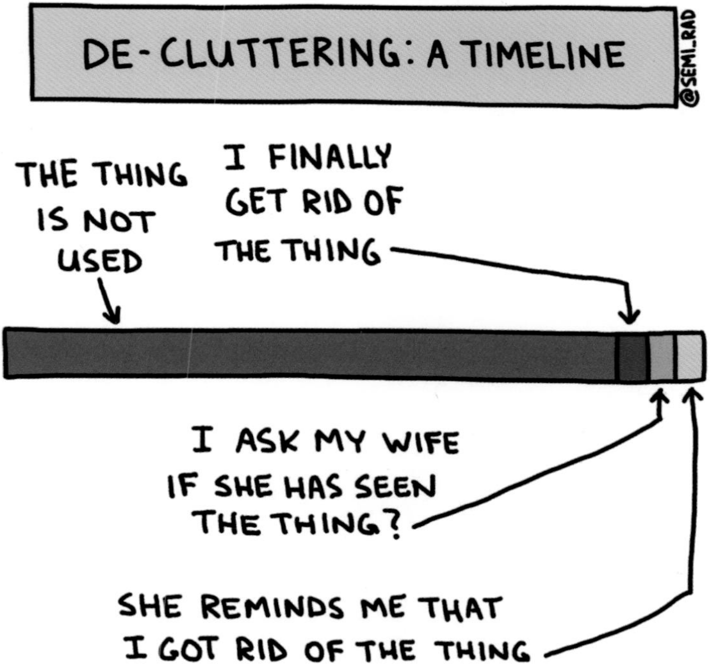
DE-CLUTTERING: A TIMELINE
@SEMI_RAD
THE THING IS NOT USED
I FINALLY GET RID OF THE THING
I ASK MY WIFE IF SHE HAS SEEN THE THING?
SHE REMINDS ME THAT I GOT RID OF THE THING

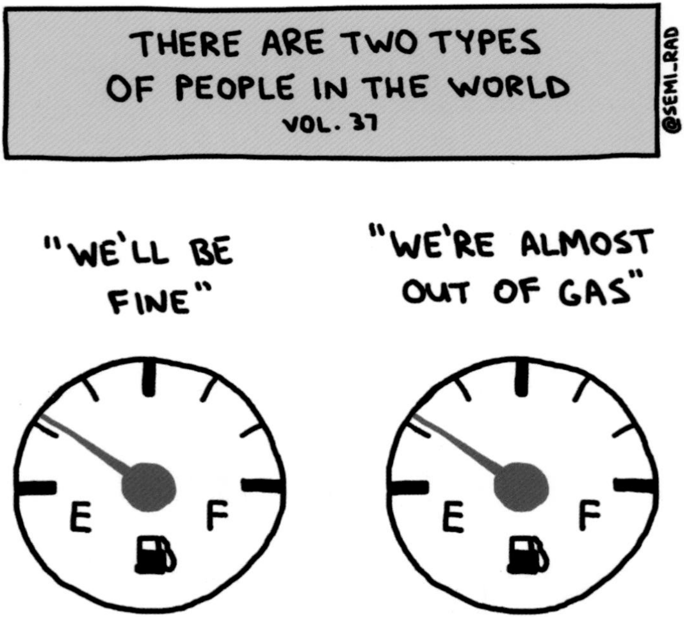
THERE ARE TWO TYPES OF PEOPLE IN THE WORLD
VOL. 37
@SEMI_RAD
"WE'LL BE FINE"
"WE'RE ALMOST OUT OF GAS"
E
F
E
F

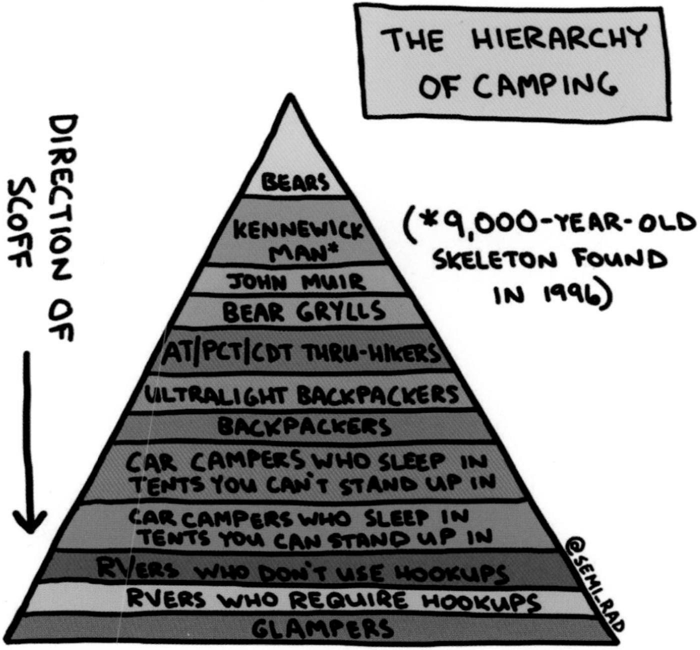
THE HIERARCHY OF CAMPING
DIRECTION OF SCOFF
BEARS
KENNEWICK MAN*
JOHN MUIR
BEAR GRYLLS
AT/PCT/CDT THRU-HIKERS
ULTRALIGHT BACKPACKERS
BACKPACKERS
CAR CAMPERS WHO SLEEP IN TENTS YOU CAN'T STAND UP IN
CAR CAMPERS WHO SLEEP IN TENTS YOU CAN STAND UP IN
RVERS WHO DON'T USE HOOKUPS
RVERS WHO REQUIRE HOOKUPS
GLAMPERS
(*9,000-YEAR-OLD SKELETON FOUND IN 1996)
@SEMI_RAD

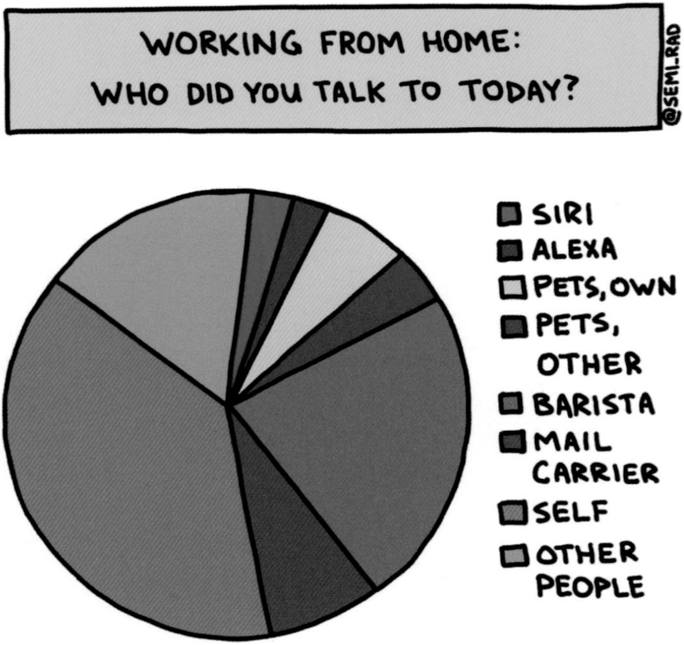
WORKING FROM HOME:
WHO DID YOU TALK TO TODAY?
@SEMI_RAD
SIRI
ALEXA
PETS, OWN
PETS, OTHER
BARISTA
MAIL CARRIER
SELF
OTHER PEOPLE

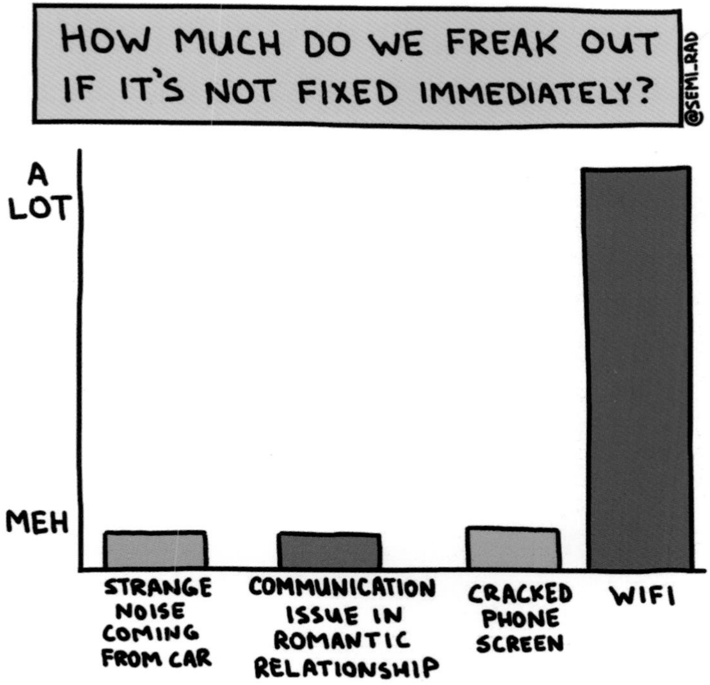
HOW MUCH DO WE FREAK OUT IF IT'S NOT FIXED IMMEDIATELY?
@SEMI_RAD
A LOT
MEH
STRANGE NOISE COMING FROM CAR
COMMUNICATION ISSUE IN ROMANTIC RELATIONSHIP
CRACKED PHONE SCREEN
WIFI

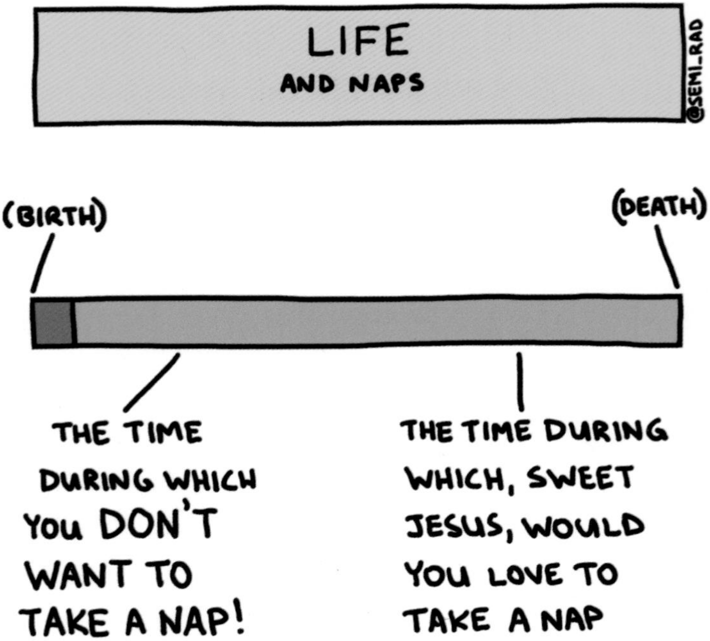
LIFE
AND NAPS
@SEMI_RAD
(BIRTH)
(DEATH)
THE TIME DURING WHICH YOU DON'T WANT TO TAKE A NAP!
THE TIME DURING WHICH, SWEET JESUS, WOULD YOU LOVE TO TAKE A NAP

4 STEPS TO REMEMBERING NAMES WHEN MEETING NEW PEOPLE AT AN EVENT

@SEMI_RAD

1. SHAKE THE PERSON'S HAND
2. REPEAT THEIR NAME BACK TO THEM ("GREAT TO MEET YOU, BOB")
3. IMMEDIATELY FORGET THE PERSON'S NAME
4. INTENTLY EAVESDROP/LISTEN FOR SOMEONE ELSE TO SAY THE PERSON'S NAME, FOR HOURS IF NECESSARY

A GRAMMATICALLY INCORRECT LIST OF UTAH'S NATIONAL PARKS

@SEMI_RAD

- ZION'S NATIONAL PARK
- ARCH'S NATIONAL PARK
- CANYONLAND'S NATIONAL PARK
- BRYCE'S CANYON'S NATIONAL PARK
- CAPITOL'S REEF'S NATIONAL PARK

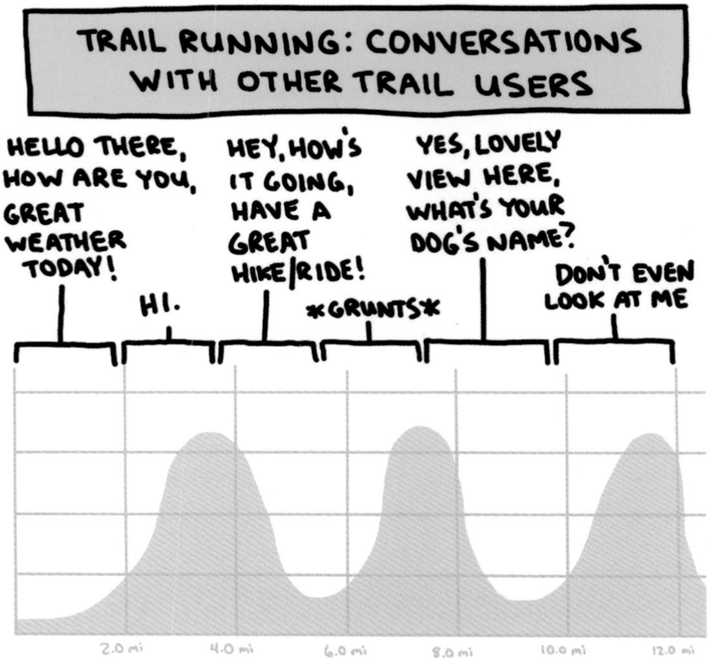

TRAIL RUNNING: CONVERSATIONS WITH OTHER TRAIL USERS
HELLO THERE, HOW ARE YOU, GREAT WEATHER TODAY!
HI.
HEY, HOW'S IT GOING, HAVE A GREAT HIKE/RIDE!
GRUNTS
YES, LOVELY VIEW HERE, WHAT'S YOUR DOG'S NAME?
DON'T EVEN LOOK AT ME
2.0 mi
4.0 mi
6.0 mi
8.0 mi
10.0 mi
12.0 mi

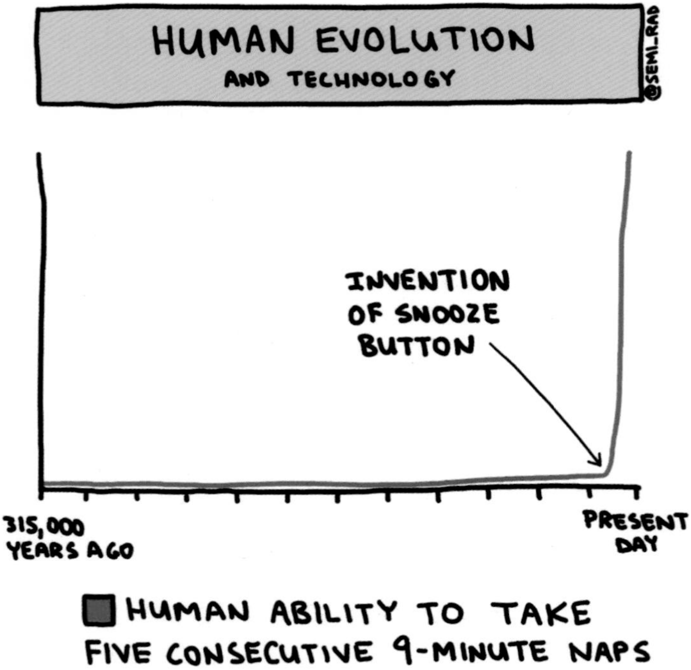
HUMAN EVOLUTION
AND TECHNOLOGY
@SEMI_RAD
INVENTION OF SNOOZE BUTTON
315,000 YEARS AGO
PRESENT DAY
HUMAN ABILITY TO TAKE FIVE CONSECUTIVE 9-MINUTE NAPS

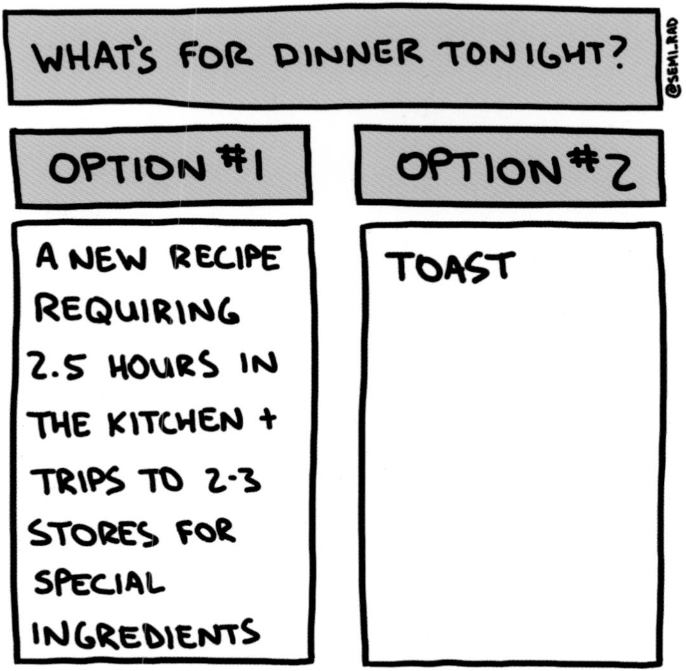
WHAT'S FOR DINNER TONIGHT?
@SEMI_RAD
OPTION #1
OPTION #2
A NEW RECIPE REQUIRING 2.5 HOURS IN THE KITCHEN + TRIPS TO 2-3 STORES FOR SPECIAL INGREDIENTS
TOAST

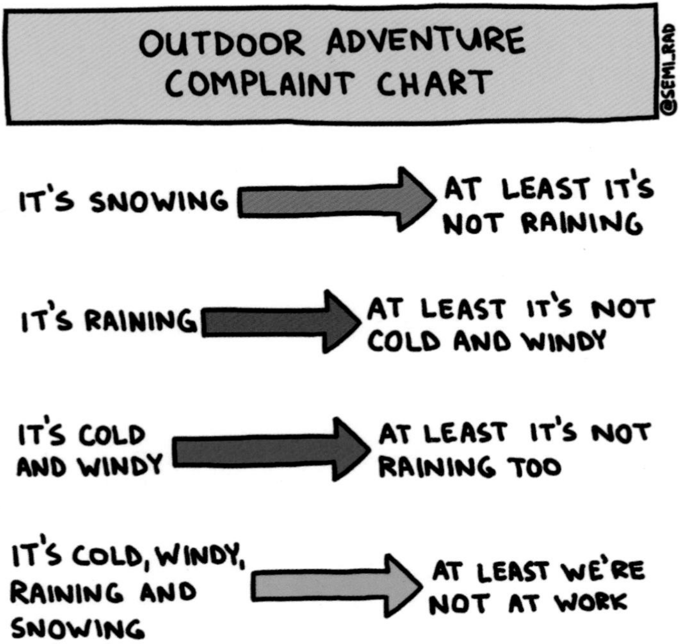
OUTDOOR ADVENTURE COMPLAINT CHART
@SEMI_RAD
IT'S SNOWING
AT LEAST IT'S NOT RAINING
IT'S RAINING
AT LEAST IT'S NOT COLD AND WINDY
IT'S COLD AND WINDY
AT LEAST IT'S NOT RAINING TOO
IT'S COLD, WINDY, RAINING AND SNOWING
AT LEAST WE'RE NOT AT WORK

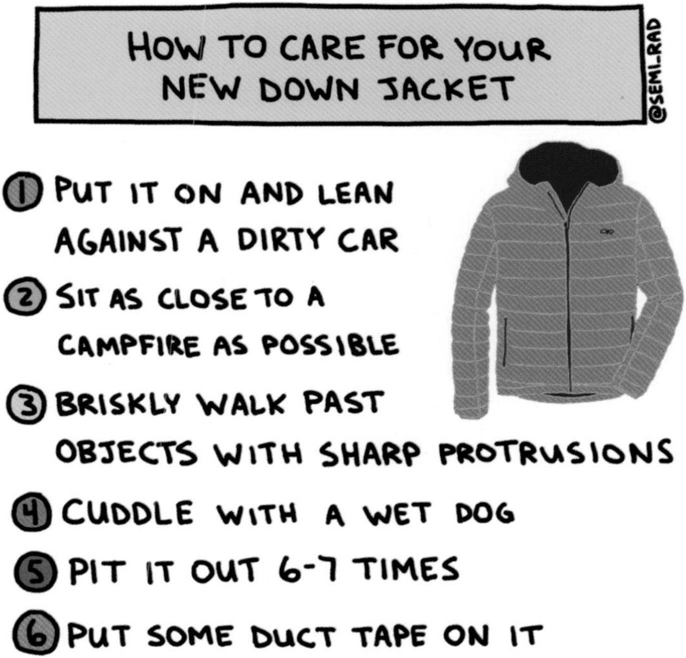
HOW TO CARE FOR YOUR NEW DOWN JACKET
@SEMI_RAD
1 PUT IT ON AND LEAN AGAINST A DIRTY CAR
2 SIT AS CLOSE TO A CAMPFIRE AS POSSIBLE
3 BRISKLY WALK PAST OBJECTS WITH SHARP PROTRUSIONS
4 CUDDLE WITH A WET DOG
5 PIT IT OUT 6-7 TIMES
6 PUT SOME DUCT TAPE ON IT

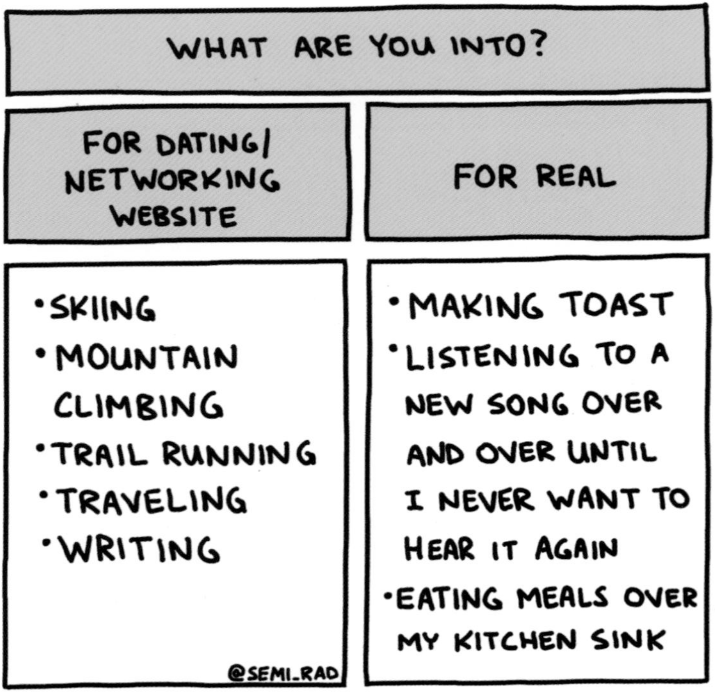
WHAT ARE YOU INTO?
FOR DATING/ NETWORKING WEBSITE
FOR REAL
• SKIING
• MOUNTAIN CLIMBING
• TRAIL RUNNING
• TRAVELING
• WRITING
• MAKING TOAST
• LISTENING TO A NEW SONG OVER AND OVER UNTIL I NEVER WANT TO HEAR IT AGAIN
• EATING MEALS OVER MY KITCHEN SINK
@SEMI_RAD

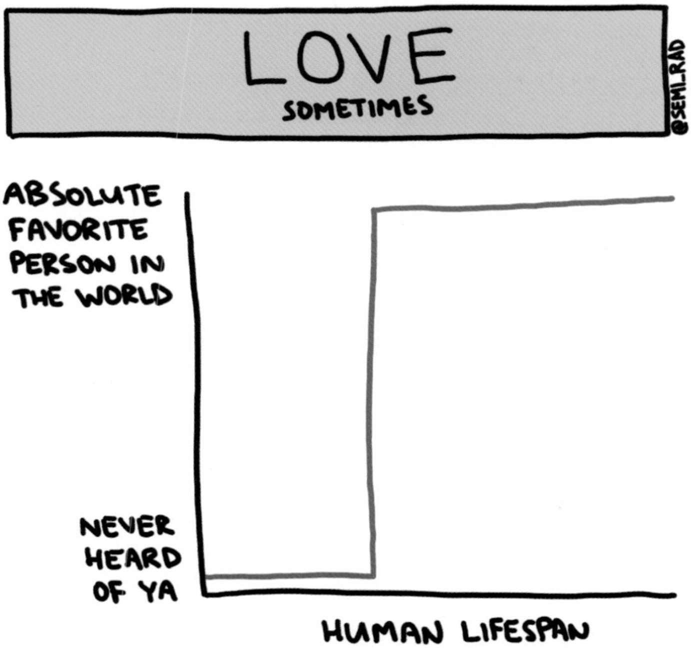
LOVE
SOMETIMES
@SEMI_RAD
ABSOLUTE FAVORITE PERSON IN THE WORLD
NEVER HEARD OF YA
HUMAN LIFESPAN

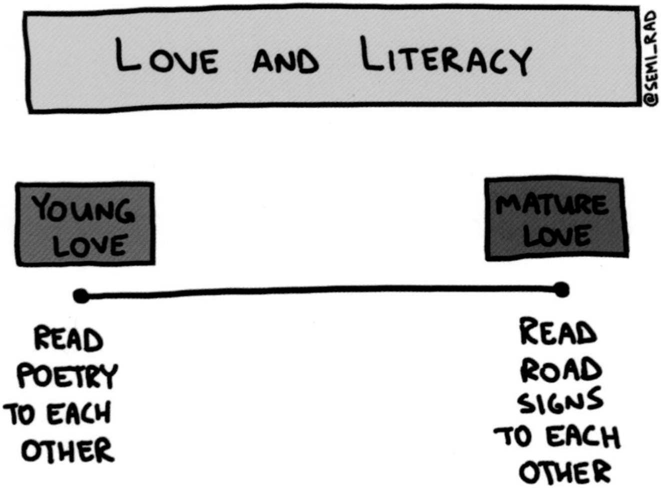
LOVE AND LITERACY
@SEMI_RAD
YOUNG LOVE
MATURE LOVE
READ POETRY TO EACH OTHER
READ ROAD SIGNS TO EACH OTHER

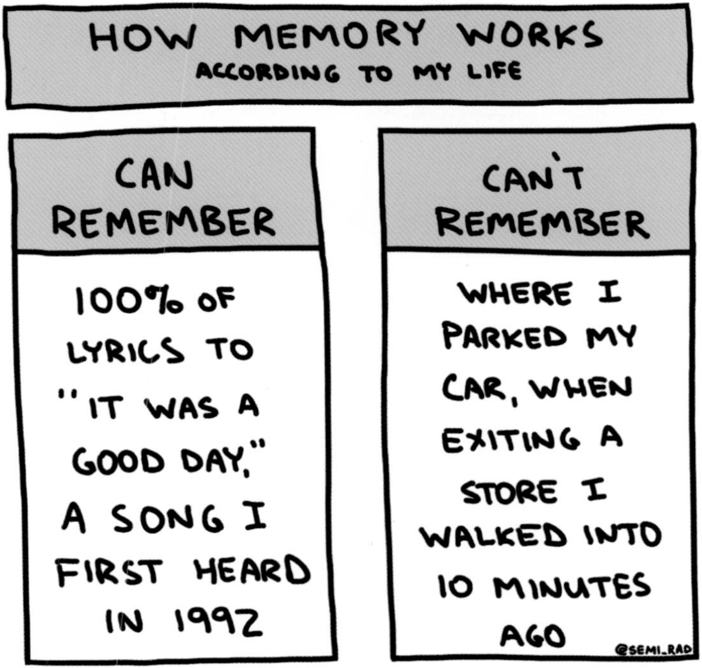
HOW MEMORY WORKS
ACCORDING TO MY LIFE
CAN REMEMBER
100% OF LYRICS TO "IT WAS A GOOD DAY," A SONG I FIRST HEARD IN 1992
CAN'T REMEMBER
WHERE I PARKED MY CAR, WHEN EXITING A STORE I WALKED INTO 10 MINUTES AGO
@SEMI_RAD

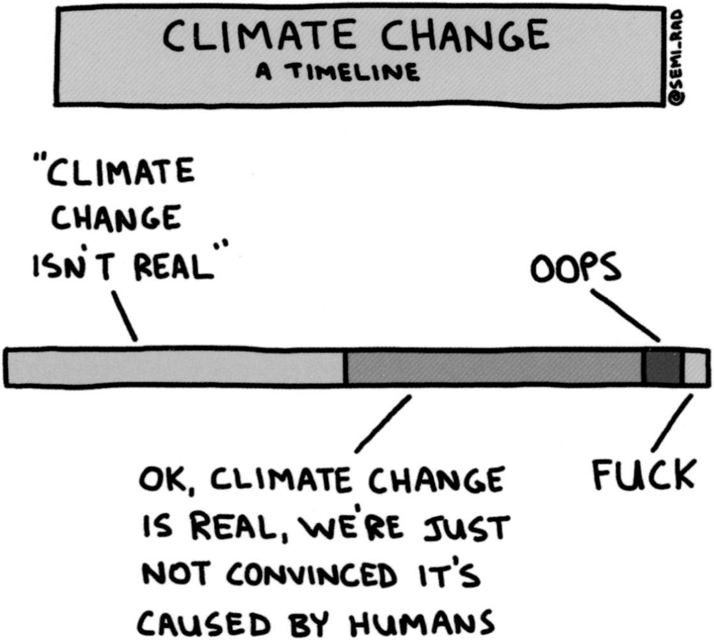
CLIMATE CHANGE
A TIMELINE
@SEMI_RAD
"CLIMATE CHANGE ISN'T REAL"
OOPS
OK, CLIMATE CHANGE IS REAL, WE'RE JUST NOT CONVINCED IT'S CAUSED BY HUMANS
FUCK

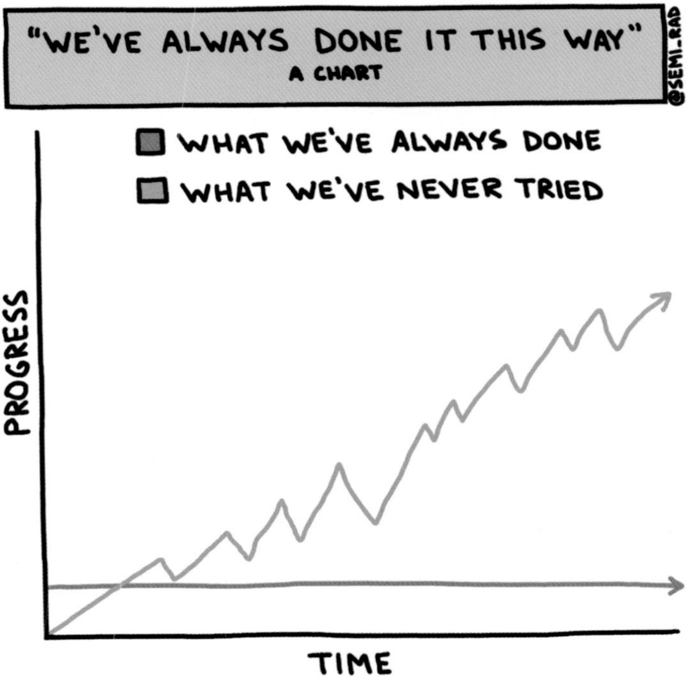
"WE'VE ALWAYS DONE IT THIS WAY"
A CHART
@SEMI_RAD
WHAT WE'VE ALWAYS DONE
WHAT WE'VE NEVER TRIED
PROGRESS
TIME

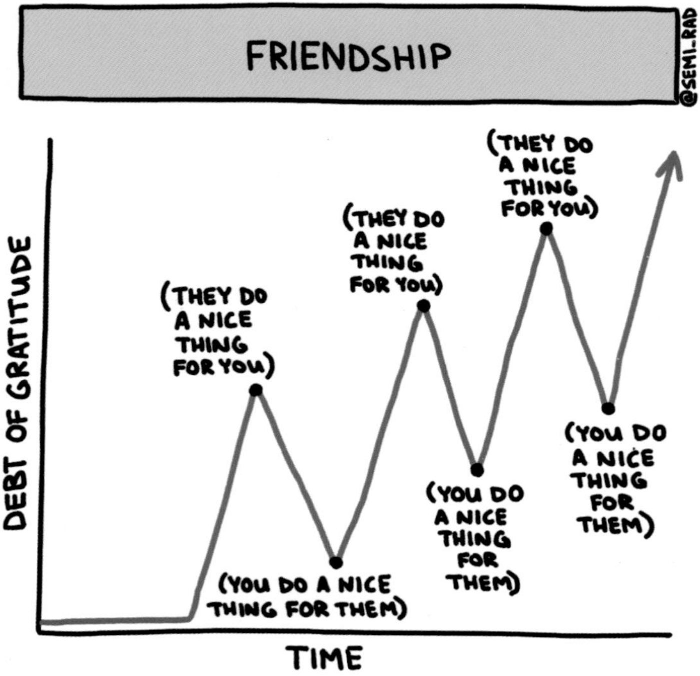

FRIENDSHIP
@SEMI_RAD
DEBT OF GRATITUDE
TIME
(THEY DO A NICE THING FOR YOU)
(YOU DO A NICE THING FOR THEM)
(THEY DO A NICE THING FOR YOU)
(YOU DO A NICE THING FOR THEM)
(THEY DO A NICE THING FOR YOU)
(YOU DO A NICE THING FOR THEM)

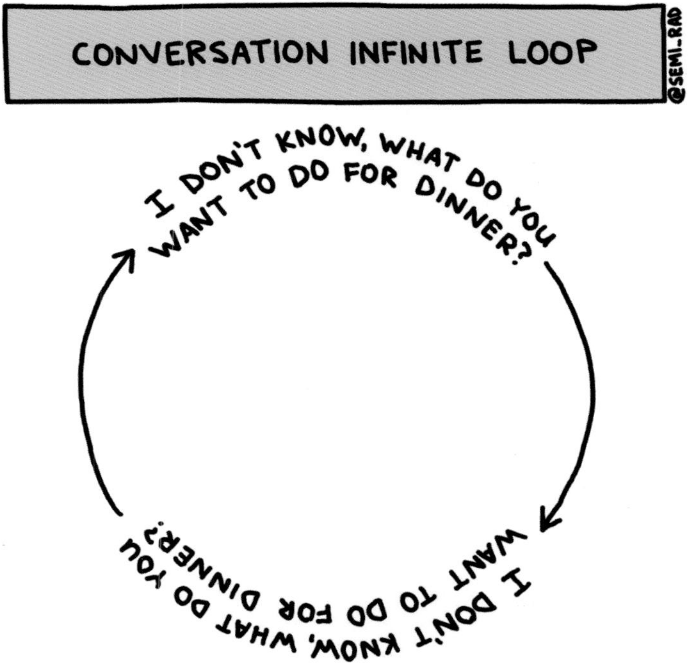
CONVERSATION INFINITE LOOP
@SEMI_RAD
I DON'T KNOW, WHAT DO YOU WANT TO DO FOR DINNER?
I DON'T KNOW, WHAT DO YOU WANT TO DO FOR DINNER?